IMPR BABLE CAUSE

The War on Terror's Assault on the Bill of Rights

Sharia Mayfield and Brandon Mayfield

DIVERTIR
PUBLISHING
Salem, NH

Improbable Cause

Sharia Mayfield and Brandon Mayfield

Copyright © 2015 by Sharia Mayfield
and Brandon Mayfield

Cover design by Kenneth Tupper

Published by Divertir Publishing LLC
PO Box 232
North Salem, NH 03073
http://www.divertirpublishing.com/

ISBN-13: 978-1-938888-12-0
ISBN-10: 1-938888-12-X

Library of Congress Control Number: 2015945354

Printed in the United States of America

Dedication and Acknowledgments

Dedicated to my wife and family (including those one step ahead of us but no longer with us), those attorneys working quietly and persistently for justice, often without thanks or praise, the judges who uphold justice, and all those men and women wrongfully oppressed or unjustly imprisoned who hang on with hope against all hope that they will one day be free.

Brandon Mayfield

Special thanks to Divertir Publishing, Gui, and everyone else who helped make our idea for a book a reality.

Sharia Mayfield

Contents

Letter from the Author, Sharia Mayfield

I n May, 2004, my father was wrongfully arrested as the alleged master-mind behind the 2004 Madrid Train Bombings—the deadliest terrorist attack since 9/11. With little more than a faulty fingerprint match to its credit, the FBI secured an affidavit for my father's arrest. While he was eventually released and the FBI admitted to its "mistake," our family was left shaken, humiliated, and paranoid. We wondered how the government could have made such a massive mistake that, in a worst-case scenario, could have earned my dad the death penalty. We wondered why the FBI had insisted on suppressing evidence of my father's innocence, particularly the Spanish Police's claims that his fingerprint was not a match to the one found near the detonation site in Spain. We wondered why there was so much mention of my father's Muslim affiliations and associations in an affidavit provided to the court, as if to imply that being Muslim was incriminating in and of itself. And most importantly, we wondered which laws authorized the government to conduct secret investigations and testify in a secret court without my father present to defend himself.

Following the tragic 9/11 attacks, America allowed for the curtail-ment of our constitutional rights with rampant support for war, expansion of governmental surveillance, and religious profiling. These reactions were not entirely without reason. Anyone under the auspices of fear and terror would likely react the same. Unfortunately, rash decisions bear long-term consequences, and we are left piecing together our shattered rights. Just as strict constitutionalists have forewarned, reducing civil liberties during crises leads to a permanent diminution of our freedom alongside an increasing executive power. This can be best described as a "one-way ratchet." [1]

Sadly, we are in a perpetual national crisis, now that the definition of armed conflict has been expanded so as to exist even when no set territo-ries are involved, no one nation has wronged us specifically, and no end is in sight. Legislation like the Patriot Act and Authorization for Use of Military Force have allowed for mass surveillance and extrajudicial killings (i.e.

without any prior judicial review). Today, still gripped with fear, people justify these measures as a necessary evil in fighting "terrorism."

Fear has led to the very thing the Constitution was to protect against—erosion of our liberties when we need them the most. If our Constitution cannot absorb the shock of a national crisis, cannot withstand the bows and slings of threats and terror, then what do we have to be proud of? What makes this country worthy of the honorable title of "Land of the Free and Home of the Brave" if we so readily make exceptions to our rights under the guise of fighting a foreign enemy?

This is the "War on Terror." We cannot let terror conquer us, however. Throughout this book, I do what I can to implore you to defend our constitutional rights and to see the myriad civil rights breaches that can occur once we cease to. I ask you to valiantly and bravely stand for the liberties that make a country great: freedom to practice religion without being persecuted, freedom from unreasonable surveillance and searches, and freedom from undue process, among others. Without public outcry, these rights—and by extension, more innocent citizens like my father—will continue to be collateral damage in the "War on Terror."

§ § §

Authors' Note: The following chapters and information provided therein are based on court records, relevant sources, and the best recollection of Brandon Mayfield (and in some instances, those who have volunteered their own recollections, including family members). While we have tried our best to verify dialogues and interactional details as much as possible, please do not confuse artistic license for objective reality. We apologize in advance for any possible errors.

§ § §

[1] *See generally* Moe and Howell, *The Presidential Power of Unilateral Action*, 15 J.L. Econ. And Org. 132 (1999).

Chapter 1
May 6, 2004

"There is no greater tyranny than that which is perpetrated
under the shield of the law and in the name of justice."
Montesquieu, *The Spirit of the Laws.*

Somebody must have framed Brandon Mayfield, for without having
done anything wrong he was arrested, shackled, and chained one
fine morning.

There were no signs of foul play in his office except for a loose gray tile
on the ceiling, attached tenuously to its designated square spot. Mr. Mayfield
had noticed it a few weeks earlier and wrote it off as nothing more than
structural deterioration. "I'll fix it later" he told himself, knowing he had
no time for minor repairs. Juggling a career, a family, and personal ambitions
(namely, philosophical musings) left him perpetually busy. He would work
all day only to come home, play with the kids, eat, sleep, wake up, take the
kids to school and repeat. Still, he was happy with his life and believed that
the constant demands kept him young and invigorated. No signs on his face
told of age—no drooping lids over his blue eyes, no wrinkles, and no grays.
At 37, he had no complaints.

As Brandon Mayfield came into his law office, nestled in the thick ferns
and pines of Portland's West Slope hills, he was not expecting any surprises.
He slumped down into a comfortable, black swivel chair, rolled up the
sleeves of his blue dress shirt, and checked nervously for voicemails or
faxes. No messages. No faxes. Nothing. It was only mildly disappointing
that the locally renowned lawyer he had reached out to the day before
was probably not interested in joining him on a wrongful death suit; what
bothered Brandon more was that the lawyer had not bothered to respond.

Resigned to take the case on alone, Brandon was about to start drafting
a brief when the phone rang. Of course, there was always some interruption
just as he was getting over a writer's block. Brandon hesitated a moment,

fingers suspended above the keyboard, before swiveling to the left and pulling the phone off the hook. What if it was the lawyer?

"Hello, Mayfield law office," he answered with more animism than usual.

"Hey, sweetie. It's me. I'm going to be late today. Got to finish cleaning up the house." It was his wife and part-time legal assistant, Mona. She usually came into the two-room office an hour after he arrived and left early to pick up the kids from school.

"Oh, wasn't expecting you. That's fine. I'm just working on a brief anyway," he said.

"Ok, I'll see you later then," she said.

"See you later, Insha'Allah." God willing.

Brandon reclined back into his seat, rested his hands on the nape of his neck and stared up at the droopy tile on the ceiling. What if it fell off and landed right on his head? Who even thought of ceiling tiles to begin with? He really should have fixed it by now.

At about a quarter to ten, Brandon was startled by an unexpected knock. He counted three loud thumps as he jumped up, maneuvered around his crammed office, past the grey filing cabinets, and to the door. He thought it was probably his neighbor, there again to tell him his mail ended up in the wrong cubby. But instead, there were two unfamiliar figures standing in the doorway. In dark business suits, they appeared to be missionaries of some sort: a thin, pale woman with a thin nose and a bulkier man with a crew cut.

"Look, whatever it is I'm not interested," Brandon said as he reached to close the door. But it became clear rather quickly that they were not missionaries or solicitors. His eyes wandered to their hips and he fixed his gaze momentarily on their holstered guns.

"We're agents of the Federal Bureau of Investigation and we're here to ask you some questions," the male agent said as he shoved through the doorway. Brandon flung his left arm out over his gray file cabinets without thinking.

"I don't want you in my office. You are in a law office which contains my client files, confidential client files that you have no business being around. I don't want to talk with you." He stood firm with his arm still outstretched and his knees locked.

"We're going to have to ask you to cooperate by answering our questions."

Brandon had no such plans. He thought back to a lecture he had attended a couple years earlier, shortly after moving to Portland. It was given by an outspoken East Coast lawyer, Stanley Cohen, and detailed how Muslim-Americans ought to respond to the FBI if they were ever confronted. Cohen was a lean man with curly dark hair and a cool sort of confidence. There was one resounding message that rang in Brandon's head: "Just say no. If the FBI wants to talk to you, it's not because they're your friends."

Coming back to the moment, Brandon found his own courage to resist their interrogation and responded more admonishingly, "If you have any questions then put them to me in writing. I am not answering any questions now and I am going to have to ask you to leave." His words hung momentarily in the air and fell on deaf ears. No one budged.

"We have a warrant for your arrest and a search warrant for your office."

Brandon stood motionless. A warrant? For his arrest? Within seconds, he felt writhing fingers sliding along his body.

"Hands out," the agent demanded before proceeding to frisk his sides, under-arms, and legs, paying special attention to his empty pockets. This must be a mistake, Brandon surmised. But they did not stop. He stood as if nailed to an invisible crucifix and evaded eye contact with the male agent, his disgust realized only in a visibly upset expression.

A strange thought came to Brandon in that moment. As he was being searched, and while avoiding any intimacy with the man in front of him, he looked up one more time at the drooping tile on the ceiling. Except, this time, he did not see a drooping tile. He saw his worst nightmare coming to life. Could it be? He dared not finish the thought. His mind trailed off on all the coincidences. He recalled seeing a dusty footprint on his desk many weeks ago, on the same day that his oldest son, Shane, came in to fix the desktop computer. Brandon insisted that Shane must have inadvertently stepped on the desk while working on the monitor underneath. It did not make much sense, but he had no other explanation. Now that he was being arrested, it retrospectively seemed fantastical but possible: he was being spied on all along. There was a small recording device hidden above the tile and his computer malfunctioned because the FBI had tampered with it—and the footstep was not his son's after all.

Brandon's mind raced and all these thoughts coalesced into a physical dizziness. He felt weak in the face of his impending fate and could find no strength, mentally or physically, to resist.

"Hands behind your back," the male agent said. That's when Brandon heard it, something he recognized only from cop shows and action movies. But in real life it sounded much more haunting: the clanking of swinging metal. The clickity-clack echoed in his head as the man grabbed Brandon's lifeless arms and pulled them back. A shooting pain stung his left shoulder as he struggled to adjust to the uncomfortable contortion, but it was useless. The cuffs snapped onto his wrists and choked them so tightly that it was impossible to slide them more than a couple inches up.

Despite his confusion, he never asked why he was being arrested. Perhaps it was because he did not want to give them the satisfaction of asking the much anticipated question. Or maybe it was because of the feeling deep down that he knew this would come, that he was being arrested and his law office was being searched and turned upside down because he was a Muslim lawyer. He associated with Muslims and represented Muslim clients; that was his "crime."

"Do you have any weapons on you? Any sharp objects in your pockets? Where are your keys?"

The questions came at him rapid-fire, and all he could say was, "No, no weapons."

The female agent, the diminutive "good cop," slapped her business card on the desk in front of Brandon and introduced herself. The male agent, who did not have a business card, identified himself as well. Brandon made a mental note to remember the names.

The female agent repeated, as if to reassure herself that what they were doing was authorized, "We have a subpoena ordering you to appear before a grand jury, an arrest warrant, and a search warrant for your office." Inside, Brandon became anxious as to what the allegations were, but a dull ache in his left shoulder prevented him from fully focusing. On the one hand, he wanted to ask the agent to reposition his arms in front to ease the pain; on the other, he did not want to appear weak. It was as though some primal urge had overtaken him and he could not, as a matter of some unspoken "man code," admit to being in pain.

The male agent chimed in that he would read the search warrant for Brandon's office, a long and detailed laundry-list of potential items to be searched for and seized. It included repeated references to bomb-making materials, which alarmed Brandon, but seemed mildly comical. Brandon barely had room in his office to turn around without bumping into something, and they expected to find blasting caps, fuses, and explosives in there? He concluded that it must have been standard language in search warrants, an example of a rigid and inflexible approach.

Brandon then turned defensive and demanded answers. "Who authorized this arrest and search warrant?" He wanted to know the man, the judge, behind this unwelcomed intrusion into his office. There was no doubt that whatever was happening to him was a mistake, and he could not even fathom remotely having committed an actual crime, much less one worthy of arrest. If only he could put a name to the man responsible for this then he could start to understand.

The female agent, with her spindly fingers, placed a copy of the affidavit in support of the warrant on the desk. Arms immobilized, Brandon—with no lack of finesse and some difficulty—managed to turn it around and maneuver it to the edge of the desk behind him. When he had it positioned correctly, he turned and bent down with his glasses just inches above the paper and glanced directly at the bottom line. That's all he wanted to know. There, in dried ink, was the autograph of the man who signed away his freedom and liberty: Federal Judge Robert Jones.

Brandon had first heard of Judge Jones while teaching a class for paralegals at the local College of Legal Arts several years ago. He had even admired and referenced Jones' decision to allow physician-assisted suicides to continue being legal in the face of federal opposition. Brandon did not know Judge Jones personally, but he felt a deep sense of betrayal, a severed membership from the fraternity of Oregon judges and lawyers—an excommunication of a sort. Any arrest, justified or not, was sure to ruin his reputation and any credibility or status he had acquired over the years. No matter what the outcome, he knew that his life would never be the same from then on.

If Brandon had been less scatterbrained, he would have known immediately that something was amiss about his arrest. But it was just starting to come to him in the form of an undeveloped intuition. There was something off in the process, in the warrant itself. Something he had learned years ago in law school as a wide-eyed man with dreams to shake the world. He thought back to a segment on constitutional guarantees. Almost. But it was more specific. More important. Something to do with cause. *Probable cause.* Yes, that was it. Probable cause. There was no probable cause that a crime had been committed, let alone that he had committed it. And no probable cause meant no Fourth Amendment rights.

The warrant recitation dragged on, "all items searched and seized will be subject to an inventory..." Brandon reflexively interrupted, regaining some autonomy, despite his physical constraint. "If you are going to search and inventory my office I want to be here to make sure it's done properly." He, having done nothing wrong, was afraid they might try to plant something in his office.

The agents seemed rather amused at this request and said flatly, "That's not an option. A team of others will be conducting the search and inventory. There will also be searches of your house and automobiles. We're going to the federal courthouse."

"My house and cars? Where are the search warrants for that?" He objected.

"It's exactly the same as the one here." The agent said as he pointed to a paper in his hand, but Brandon paid no attention. To him it was all illegal anyway. He had done nothing wrong. There was no cause, let alone probable cause, that he had done anything criminal.

The male agent, before escorting Brandon outside, asked again where the car keys were so that he could search Brandon's '94 Chevy Corsica.

He replied, "You actually expect me to tell you?"

"Either that or we'll just break a window," he said in a matter-of-fact tone. It was pointless. The left side back door to the maroon car was broken and never fully latched on the hinge. A bit of tugging and it would snap right open anyway.

"Do whatever you have to do but I won't be complicit in this unlawful search."

The male agent then mumbled to himself that he had seen some keys on the desk that probably included the one to the car.

"Let's go see Judge Jones," Brandon demanded. "I am anxious to talk to him. I cannot believe he signed this." He was sure that this was all a big misunderstanding and with a short explanation Judge Jones would realize it, apologize, and move for his release. At least, that was what Brandon hoped for.

The male agent led the cuffed man out of the building, which was actually a refurbished apartment complex, and into the public eye. Outside, it smelled of pine and decaying carcasses, the ornamental pear trees notorious for their rancid odor. The beautiful day was menacing and the bright sunlight became a surreal haze. A whole team of agents with gloves, notepads, and briefcases headed toward the office as if they were about to perform a forcible appendectomy. Bystanders milling around, peering out from windows and stairway balconies, completed his humiliation. Some probably snickered from afar that they had seen that guy and may have even talked to him. Others probably made wild speculation as to what was happening in their otherwise eventless lives. Mr. Mayfield had become the local spectacle, the subject of detached curiosity and amusement, like a car accident on a traffic-ridden road.

Hands still cuffed, Brandon was placed in the back seat of an unmarked Ford Explorer parked outside his office building. Sitting with his arms pressed against the back of the car seat only exacerbated the pain and he finally told the male agent he had an old injury.

"Can you recuff me with my hands in front?" he pleaded, admitting, to his chagrin and deflated ego, that he was in pain. But the agent would hear none of it.

Putting his face so close to Brandon's ear that Brandon could feel his warm breath and with an intimidating voice borrowed from a bad cop show, he said, "Look me in the eye."

Brandon did not move.

"I said look me in the eye," the agent repeated through his teeth, and Brandon turned to face him. "Don't you fuck with me. Don't you dare try anything. Do you hear me? Do you understand me?"

With the meekness that arrest and being virtually immobile can create, Brandon answered, "I'm not going to try anything. I have a shoulder injury from when I was in the military and have had two surgeries before."

After asking when exactly he had the operations, the agent then commanded him to step out of the SUV. With an eye on the crowd outside, Brandon begged, "This is embarrassing and humiliating. I work here and people are watching. Could you undo the cuffs without me getting out?"

The agent responded, in a calm tone, "Oh, you don't have to worry about that. The media is right behind us."

Feeling as if he had taken yet another blow, Brandon wondered if it was routine for the FBI to make public announcements of its arrests and invite reporters along for the show. Brandon did not understand the seriousness of his alleged crime and had yet to hear exactly why he was being arrested, but he did not want to be degraded more and refused to get out of the SUV. To the agent's credit, Brandon was recuffed inside.

§ § §

The drive to the federal courthouse was quiet and uneventful. Staring out of the car window, Brandon watched the world pass by: stores, restaurants, an animal shelter, a long stretch of highway and then downtown. By then, he was calm, almost unfazed. Judge Jones would clear it all up, he thought. But he did worry about his wife and kids. How would he contact them? What would Mona do when she saw he was not in the office as planned? Or were they raiding his home at the exact same time? The last thought sent a pang of despair through his body. He did not, could not, imagine his wife being implicated in this mess that was somehow his fault.

Finally, the male agent broke the silence. Just over halfway to the courthouse, as they proceeded through the lazy traffic lights in front of Portland State University, he said in almost a whisper, "Brandon, listen very carefully to what I am about to say to you. Think long and hard about it before you decide whether to talk. Remember how the brothers stood up for Mike Hawash? They're not going to be there for you. You think about that."

Hawash was one of the Portland Seven, middle-aged local Muslims who had admitted to and were sentenced for hapless attempts to go to Afghanistan to join the Taliban. The local Muslim community had risen in his defense and was badly shaken by his subsequent confessions of guilt.

Why the hell did the agent presume Brandon knew about Mike Hawash or had any connection to the guy, Brandon mused. He continued staring out the window, pained by the predicament but careful not to respond to the agent. He was saving his defense for the judge and did not want to say anything that could be used against him somehow.

The worst part of it, of the arrest, was his surrendering all power, both physically and mentally. Only half an hour or so had passed, but Brandon was already exhausted and upset. Naively, he wished he had not opened the door earlier, that they would have mistakenly surmised he was not there or that he was running late that morning. He wished that the door's lock would have then kept them at bay as they jiggled it unsuccessfully and angrily. He wished they would have turned around and decided to come back later only to realize he was the wrong guy. The wrong guy to arrest. The wrong guy to ruin. The wrong guy to mess with.

Chapter 2
Infierno Terrorista

"The means of defense against foreign danger have been always
the instruments of tyranny at home. Among the
Romans it was a standing maxim to excite a war, whenever
a revolt was apprehended." James Madison, 1787.

"We need a common enemy to unite us. We need a new threat."
Condoleezza Rice, March, 2000.

I n November of 2003, the Associated Press published preliminary reports
that detainees held in American prisons in Iraq were being humiliated,
assaulted, beaten, and even killed. The most notorious of the prisons
was Abu Ghraib, now known as Baghdad Central Prison. While the reports
did not gain much traction, the U.S. Central Command launched an official
investigation of the military abuses in January of 2004.[1] By February, seventeen
soldiers had been suspended, and by March official charges had been
brought against six.[2]

It was not until late April, 2004, that the U.S. news magazine "60 Minutes
II" broadcasted a story on the prisoner abuses, complete with horrifying
photos illustrating the atrocities.[3] The public was soon shocked and haunted
by images of sexual assaults, beatings, and other forms of humiliation. In
one famous photo, a female soldier sports a thumbs up in front of five nude
Iraqi men whose heads are covered in black hoods. In another, a man is
forced to stand on a small box while electrical wires are attached to his
body. In yet another, naked men are forced into a human pyramid. Americans
knew that war was not always the noblest pursuit and that death and wrongdoing were inevitable, but none expected that their own military could
commit such atrocities—that soldiers, under the command of higher officials,
could treat other humans so inhumanely.

While the Abu Ghraib scandal slowly unraveled before the public eye, the world was afflicted by yet another tragedy. On March 11, 2004, thousands of unsuspecting passengers boarded four commuter trains in Madrid, Spain, departing from the station "Alcalá de Henares." What would have otherwise been an uneventful, rush-hour morning under overcast skies soon turned into a national horror. Droopy-eyed artists, students, consultants, and managers boarded the subway trains heading to school or work as usual. Some stood while others sat with their heads bowed. Some were alert, others half-asleep. Many of the passengers had seen each other on their regular morning commute, while others seemed strangers. But when ten detonators exploded at approximately 7:40 a.m., sending human bodies flying and glass shattering, no one was a stranger anymore.[4] Men and women lay strewn across the ground naked, bloodied, and dismembered. The train's cars were blackened and burned. Smoke filled the air. Frantic passengers jumped from windows to hard ground, a few cracking their skulls on their descent. As one male passenger described, as a testament to the horror:

> "I heard a girl moaning, 'Help me.' There was a big metal beam on top of her. Two other girls and a man and I got her out from under the beam. By then she wasn't conscious and I took her pulse. As I was doing that, her heart stopped. I had seen her all year on the train, but we had never talked before." [5]

But there was no time for mourning when hundreds more were in need of assistance. The man ripped the scarf from the just-deceased woman and made a make-shift tourniquet to help another man who had lost his leg below the knee.[6] Injured victims ran haplessly, crimson streaming from their noses and eyes. Other limbless victims bled to death, their silent pleas ignored by the emergency response medics trained to help the less severely injured and maximize outreach. In a more chilling recount of the events on the ground, a first-rescuer details the plight of the dying victims:

> "Inside the train there were people who were still alive but not strong enough to ask for help. They look into your eyes and you can see their eyes begging you. They have no legs. They have

no arms. But you don't help them. They're going to die. You can't save them and there are so many other people with a better chance of survival.

You can't spend too long with any one person—even one woman who was six months pregnant. I was opening up tracheas so people could breathe. Others are in hypovolemic shock, so you have to give them an IV. You can't spend more than three or four minutes with any one person and you never finish—there is always more you can do. We could hear the dead people's mobile phones. It was so shocking—these phones ringing that nobody was ever going to answer." [7]

The explosions left nearly 200 dead and another 1,800 injured and would later be deemed the "terrorist hell"—the "infierno terrorista." [8] There was simply no other way to describe the bloodshed, gore, and terror but as an inferno. News spread so quickly that by evening, millions of Americans had come to learn of the bombing. Televisions were flooded with "Breaking News" headlines and the now-infamous footage of a smoking train wreck.

§ § §

When Brandon Mayfield came home from work on March 11, 2004, he was not expecting an unordinary night. He grabbed a plate of food from the kitchen, descended one step into the cozy living room, and turned to see the breaking news. There was that infamous photo of a smoking train and already reports of hundreds of deaths and injuries. Mona, his wife, was plopped on the emerald-green sectional, eyes glued to the television. The two of them immediately shared a mutual, but unspoken, understanding. They were terrified and disgusted that anyone could kill so many innocent people. But they also wondered who had done it and why. What business did terrorists have in Spain? Was it a political statement? "Unbelievable," he said before sitting down to his dinner and flipping between the news channels. "I don't know who did this, but whoever did it are criminals of the first order. I'm sick and tired of all this senseless killing," he muttered half to himself, half to Mona.

§ § §

But even as the news was spreading, three undetonated explosives remained at large on the trains as everyone evacuated the scene. A swift police team flooded the area to investigate. In a heroic show of competence and bravery, bomb disposal professionals discovered and detonated two of the remaining explosives, and the final one was found later in the evening among train luggage. But the investigation was far from over.

Outside the "Alcalá de Henares" station, a stolen white Kangoo van was parked. Inside of it were cellphones and a plastic blue bag containing detonators. The Spanish National Police (SNP) recovered fingerprints from the plastic bag and two days later sent digital photographs of their findings to Interpol Madrid. Interpol then forwarded the prints to the FBI in Quantico, Virginia. The FBI entered the prints into a computer database in hopes of putting a finger on the mastermind behind the Madrid Train Bombings. One of the recovered prints, identified by the FBI as Latent Fingerprint #17 (LFP #17), was linked to twenty potential matches. Number four on the list? Brandon Mayfield.[9]

§ § §

[1] Ricchiardi, Sherry. "Missed Signals." American Journalism Review. Aug./ Sept. 2004. Web. 1 Sept. 2014. <http://ajrarchive.org/article.asp? id=3716>.

[2] "Intelligence." Abu Ghurayb Prison Prisoner Abuse. Web. 1 Sept. 2014. <http://www.globalsecurity.org/intell/world/iraq/abu-ghurayb-chronology.htm>.

[3] *See* supra note 1.

[4] Loewenberg, Samuel, Courtney Rubin, and Leela Landress. "Terror on a Train." *People.* 29 Mar. 2004. Vol. 61, No. 12. 64, *available at* < http:// www.people.com/people/archive/article/0,,20149665,00.html>.

[5] *Id.*

[6] *Id.*

[7] *Id.*

[8] *See* Miquel, Mathieu. "March 11, 2004 in Madrid: Was it really an Islamist attack?" Voltaire Network. 28 Nov. 2009. Web. 1 Sept. 2014. <http://www.voltairenet.org/article163076.html>

[9] *Id.*

Chapter 3
Convince the Spanish First.
The Rest Should be Easy.

"All political thinking for years past has been vitiated in the same way. People can foresee the future only when it coincides with their own wishes, and the most grossly obvious facts can be ignored when they are unwelcome." George Orwell

The March 11 Spain bombing occurred just before the March 15 elections in Spain, sparking rumors that it was politically motivated. The ruling party lost the elections, partly for its handling of the Madrid bombing. The contending Socialist Party won 42% of the vote, while the right wing Popular Party won only 38% of the vote.[1] Initially the government, under Prime Minister Jose Aznar and his Popular Party, blamed Basque separatists as the bombers.[2] That seemed to be the most plausible explanation. But the tides were quickly changing.

On the Saturday following the attack, only hours before the official elections, Spain announced its arrest of three Moroccans and two Indians.[3] At the time, this signaled that the attacks likely had nothing to do with the vote and all to do with Spain's global clout. Thousands of Spaniards took to the streets protesting the government[4] and, the next day, the Spanish voted in an unprecedented 77% voter turnout.[5] As one first-time voter stated: "It's the first time I voted. I feel very happy because the government had to change...because of the Iraq war." [6]

The Spanish people argued that Aznar's allegiance with Bush, and his assistance in America's "War on Terror," had made Spain the target of terrorist attacks. The people felt they had no business fighting a war in Iraq, and the Madrid bombing had proved their worst fears: Spain had become more vulnerable, not safer, to foreign attacks as a result of their government's involvement in the war in Iraq.[7] For this reason, Aznar and his right-leaning conservative party were reluctant to reveal that the suspects were possible Islamic extremists, likely for fear of the repercussions.

In an effort to obtain international assistance, the SNP sent digital images of fourteen latent fingerprints recovered from its investigation to INTERPOL, who forwarded the images by e-mail to the FBI on March 13, 2004.[8] Unit Chief Michael Wieners of the FBI Laboratory Latent Print Units (LPU) reported to work that Saturday to respond to the high-priority request. He requested assistance from a fellow examiner. Upon receiving higher resolution latents, the examiner compared the latent prints to a database with over 47 million candidates' prints using the FBI's Integrated Automated Fingerprint Identification System (IAFIS).[9] After comparing the original fingerprint cards, he concluded on March 16, that number four (Brandon Mayfield) candidate's left index finger matched that of Latent Fingerprint #17 (LFP #17).[10] Although two other examiners in the unit unofficially examined the prints and expressed doubts about a match, an assistant and two forensics analysts (including John Massey) verified the match. Copies of Brandon's original prints were subsequently sent to the Spanish National Police (SNP) on April 2, 2004.[11]

When the print arrived at Quantico, officials claim they asked Spain for access to the original but there was no response, and it was not clear if anyone at the FBI followed up on the request. Brandon's cards from an arrest in Wichita as a teen (detailed in Chapter 9) and from his commission in the Army were compared to the latent prints, and the FBI claimed there were an excess of 15 common points of identification.[12] After conducting their own tests, Spanish law enforcement officials had come to a different result and reported back to the FBI in an April 13 memo that the match was conclusively negative.[13]

On April 15, FBI examiners touted that they were "absolutely confident" in the match despite hearing doubts from Spanish authorities just days earlier.[14] Rather than "determine the complete basis" of the disagreement, the FBI "commit[ed] anew to the validity" of its original determination,[15] sending Wieners to meet with the Spanish National Police the following week to "explain" the FBI's basis for its match.[16] In a 2006 report, even the Office of Inspector General faulted the FBI's "overconfidence in the skill and superiority of its examiners" as preventing the FBI from taking the Spanish reports "as seriously as it should have." [17]

MINISTRY
OF THE INTERIOR

POLICE
HEADQUARTERS
FORENSIC SCIENCE
DIVISION

OFFICIAL LETTER

Your reference:

Our reference:

Madrid, 13 April, 2004

SUBJECT: **ANALYSIS AND COMPARISON OF FINGERPRINTS**

In response to your document of reference, in which you requested the analysis and comparison of three deca-dactylar cards belonging to BRANDON BIERI MAYFIELD, from the FBI Laboratory in the United States, we inform you that the Special Proceedings Sections[1] performed the appropriate studies[2] of the above mentioned, with the latent prints discovered during the different crime scene inspections carried out as a result of the 11 March, 2004 terrorist attacks investigations, as well as the deca-dactylar cards of the varied suspects that were given to this Police Precinct. The result was NEGATIVE. We also report that the fingerprints have been entered in our Automatic Dactylar Identification System for their respective study regarding matters connected to the 11 March, 2004 attacks, as well as any other criminal activity. The result was also NEGATIVE.

But what was "overconfidence" of the FBI was anathema to Brandon. Despite doubt even from Portland's FBI division that there was probable cause to arrest Brandon,[18] the government sought to do just that. On May 6, 2004, the FBI submitted affidavits to the court in support of its search and arrest warrants. The FBI conveniently did not mention the April 13 "negative" report from the SNP. Instead, the affidavits contained "several inaccuracies that reflected a regrettable lack of attention to detail." [19] For example, the FBI mentioned that a "final determination had not been rendered" by the SNP, and that the SNP had only reported "preliminary" findings that were "not consistent" with those of the FBI.[20] That the SNP's "inconsistent" and "preliminary" findings casted doubt on the FBI's purported "100% positive match" and yet were not substantiated in the arrest warrant is particularly egregious. In fact, nowhere in the affidavit did it mention the negative result the Spanish officials had come to. In addition, the FBI went so far as saying that it believed the SNP "felt satisfied" with the identification after meeting with the Unit Chief in April;[21] however, the SNP had only agreed to re-examine the identification following the meeting.[22]

"They had a justification for everything," said Pedro Luis Melida Lledo, head of the fingerprint unit for the SNP, whose team analyzed the prints in question and attended the April 21 meeting with the Unit Chief Wieners. "But I just couldn't see it." [23]

Carlos Corrales, a commissioner of the SNP's science division was also struck by the FBI's relentless insistence Brandon Mayfield's fingerprint was that of a terrorist. "It seemed as though they had something against him," Mr. Corrales said, "and they wanted to involve us." [24]

§ § §

Fingerprint matches are made by finding corresponding points of comparison between prints. From the time we are born we all have raised layers of skin with openings for sweat glands on our hands and the soles of our feet known as friction ridges. The friction ridges create unique patterns used by fingerprint examiners to match prints. To compare prints examiners must look for the places where the friction ridges join or split. If there are sufficient points of comparison a match is declared; if not a match is ruled out. If there is insufficient information, the match is found to be inconclusive.

The typical procedure known by the acronym ACE-V involves analysis of useful identifiers, comparison of the predicted key spatially located identifiers on one print to the comparison print, and evaluation of the quality and quantity and similarity of the comparative data, followed by verification from a separate examiner. One of the problems with this method is print examiners or computer matching programs generally make their determination based on analysis of only a partial print.[25] Matching partial prints to a full rolled print presents fewer details and points of comparison as well as an uncontrolled impression subject to distortions.

§ § §

[1] "Spanish government admits defeat." *BBC News.* 29 Mar. 2004. Web. 28 Feb. 2015. <http://news.bbc.co.uk/2/hi/europe/3511280.stm>

[2] "Madrid Blasts: Who is to Blame?" *BBC News.* 12 Mar. 2004. Web. 29. Aug. 2014<http://news.bbc.co.uk/2/hi/europe/3501364.stm>

[3] Sciolino, Elaine, and Lizette Alvarez. "Officials Arrest 3 Moroccans and 2 Indians." *NYT.* 14. Mar. 2004. Web. 14. Mar. 2015. <http://www.nytimes.com/2004/03/14/international/europe/14SPAI.html>

[4] *Id.*

[5] *See* supra note 1.

[6] *See id.*

[7] Cruickshank, Paul, and Peter Bergen. "Iraq 101: The Iraq Effect - The War in Iraq and Its Impact on the War on Terrorism - Pg. 1." *Mother Jones.* 1 Mar. 2007. Web. 29 Aug. 2014. <http://www.motherjones.com/politics/2007/03/iraq-101-iraq-effect-war-iraq-and-its-impact-war-terrorism-pg-1>. (By as early as 2007 estimates show that the war on Iraq increased terrorism sevenfold).

[8] "A Review of the FBI's Handling of the Brandon Mayfield Case." U.S. Department of Justice. Office of the Inspector General, March 2006. Web. 29 Aug. 2014. 29-30. <http://www.justice.gov/oig/special/s0601/final.pdf>

[9] *Id.* at 118.

[10] *Id.* at 31.

[11] See *id.* at 42, footnote 22.

[12] *Id.* at 241.

[13] *Id.* at 9.

[14] *Id.* at 10

[15] *Id.*

[16] *Id.* at 2

[17] *Id.* at 10.

[18] *Id.* at 62, footnote 36.

[19] *Id.* at 19.

[20] *Id.* at 64-65

[21] *Id.* at 244

[22] *Id.* at 19.

[23] Kershaw, Sarah. "Spain and U.S. at Odds on Mistaken Terror Arrest." *The New York Times*. The New York Times, 5 June 2004. Web. 29 Aug. 2014. <http://www.nytimes.com/2004/06/05/us/spain-and-us-at-odds-on-mistaken-terror-arrest.html?module=Search&mabReward=relbias%3Ar>

[24] *Id.*

[25] Feige, David. "Printing Problems, The inexact science of fingerprint analysis" *Slate Magazine*. Web. 27 May 2004. <www.slate.com/articles/news_and_politics/jurisprudence/2004/05/printing_problems.htm>.

Chapter 4
The Work of the Beast: Star Chambers, FISA, and the Fourth Amendment

"Democracies die behind closed doors...The framers of the First Amendment 'did not trust any government to separate the true from the false for us.' They protected the people against secret government." [1]
Judge Damon J. Keith

T he Star Chamber was an English court of law that operated from the late 1400's to 1641, when it was abolished after the severe mistreatment of several religious dissenters. The court at the royal palace of Westminster was made up of a number of privy councilors and common law judges. The court, as a supplement to the courts in civil and criminal matters, was set up to ensure enforcement of laws against people that ordinary courts would have difficulty in convicting of their crimes. The court sessions were held in secret with no writing and no witnesses. It has come to be looked back upon as a regrettable example of misuse and abuse of power by the English monarchy and courts.

The Star Chamber was abolished by an act of Parliament known as the Habeas Corpus Act of 1640. The man most responsible for its demise was John Lilburne. He was brought before the members of the Star Chamber for unlicensed publishing,[2] but instead of being charged was asked how he would plead. In his examination, he refused to take the oath on the ground that he was not bound to incriminate himself, stating that: "I have a right to know what this inquisition is about before I place my soul at risk by swearing before God to tell the truth in response to any and all irrelevant questions." [3] For his refusal to cooperate, he was publicly whipped, dragged by his hands tied to the rear of an ox cart, then gagged and thrown in prison.[4] While in prison he wrote and published an account of his treatment, entitled "The Work of the Beast." [5] Lilburne's ordeal has been cited by jurists and scholars as the historical foundations of the Fifth Amendment.

No secret court has formally been authorized in America prior to 1978.[6] The U.S. Constitution makes no provision for such courts, and virtually every state constitution guarantees open and public courts.[7] For example, Oregon's Constitution, article 1, section 10, states that "No court shall be secret, but justice shall be administered openly and without purchase." The Fourth Amendment, which has served us well for nearly 200 years, was altered under the guise that it was necessary to make us safer. In 1978, Congress passed the Foreign Intelligence Surveillance Act (FISA) act, carving out for the first time an exception to the Fourth Amendment's probable cause requirement. By this act, Congress authorized America's very own Star Chamber, the first secret American court, known as the Foreign Intelligence Surveillance Court—a secret court whose purpose is to grant secret search and surveillance warrants and orders.

Before the FISA the, U.S. Supreme Court, in *Katz v. U.S.*, was asked to determine whether the Fourth Amendment probable cause requirement applied to surveillance of phone conversations and ruled that it did.[8] Charles Katz was a Los Angeles bookie who used a public pay phone booth to transmit illegal gambling bets to Miami and Boston. Without his knowledge the FBI was recording his conversations by means of an electronic eavesdropping devise attached to the exterior of the phone booth. Congress, in response, passed Title III of the Omnibus Crime Control and Safe Streets Act of 1968, codifying *Katz* and requiring a determination of probable cause by a federal judge before the government could perform electronic surveillance of phone conversations.

In 1972, the Supreme Court was asked to determine if such a requirement applied to foreign intelligence purposes or was subject to the national security exception of probable cause requirements. The court ruled there was to be no exception to the Fourth Amendment requirement of advance judicial authorization for internal domestic surveillance and recommended that Congress adopt a different standard for strictly foreign intelligence gathering.[9]

In the 1979 Supreme Court case *Smith v. Maryland*, the court rejected the idea that the installation and use of a pen register (an electronic device that records all numbers from a particular phone line) constituted a violation of one's "legitimate expectation of privacy" since the numbers would be available to and recorded by the phone company anyway. The court had earlier (in *U.S. v. Miller*, 1976) also rejected any right to privacy for bank records since such information is willingly provided to third parties. However, Justice Sotomayor, in a concurring opinion (in *U.S. v. Jones*, 2012), recently noted that in today's digital age "it may be necessary to reconsider the premise that an individual has no reasonable expectation of privacy regarding information voluntarily disclosed to third parties."

Around the same time that the Supreme Court was faced with the new challenge of advancing privacy policies alongside digital innovation, the U.S. was faced with its own challenge. During the Cold War, political dissidents were targeted for surveillance by the government as suspected communists. The practice of illegally wiretapping and eavesdropping on suspected political dissidents is looked back upon as "McCarthyism." Well into the 60's, members of the Nation of Islam and the Black Panther movement were also targeted for surveillance, and in perhaps a more notorious example, even Dr. Martin Luther King Jr. fell prey to the auspices of FBI spying. As a result of the rampant abuses of government power and an unclear stance from the Supreme Court as to what was acceptable spying practice, in 1975 Congress created the Church Commission to investigate and suggest change. The committee described the unlawful government surveillance as "vacuum cleaners sweeping in information about lawful activities of American citizens." [10]

In response to recommendations of the Church Commission, Congress passed the FISA Act, which permitted the government to get an electronic surveillance order based on probable cause that a target was a foreign power or agent of a foreign power. The proponent had to certify that "the purpose" was to gather foreign intelligence information. FISA was a compromise aimed at protecting the American public from government over-intrusion while still allowing for narrow but important foreign intelligence gathering. A number of U.S. appellate cases both pre- and post-FISA held that warrantless searches were all right so long as the "primary purpose" was to gather strictly "foreign" intelligence, and any evidence of criminal activity was incidental.

The threat that the passage of the FISA Act and the creation of a secret court poses to our civil liberties is critical. Prior to 1978, the general consensus amongst the courts since the adoption of our Bill of Rights was that, for ordinary criminal investigations, communications interception was viewed as a grave intrusion on the rights of privacy and speech. Up until the passage of FISA, the authority and command of the Fourth Amendment's requirement that "no warrant shall issue but upon probable cause" (that a crime has been committed) remained absolute. Unfortunately, FISA carved out a small yet dangerous exception to the probable cause requirement when it permitted surveillance based on a finding of probable cause that the surveillance target is a foreign power or an agent of a foreign power. This is a subtle but important difference. In one instance the government cannot get a warrant unless it swears with particularity who it will arrest, or what it will search, and that there is probable cause that a crime has been committed. On the other hand, after FISA was enacted, a government official could go to a secret court with an application for a secret warrant and swear that there was probable cause to believe a surveillance target was a foreign power or an agent of a foreign power, irrespective of whether any crime had been committed.

FISA, in order to give assurance to the public that this was not an example of oppressive government but merely a means to strengthen our intelligence gathering capabilities, ensured that none of the information gathered under such surveillance could under any circumstances ever be used for a criminal trial. The secret FISA court was not to grant a search warrant unless the applicant asserted that the primary purpose was to gather foreign intelligence. Of course it was only a matter of time before that safeguard, between foreign intelligence gathering and domestic criminal investigation, would be removed. September 11 was the perfect excuse to do just that, and in the wake of the terrifying attacks, the Patriot Act was passed.

Section 218 of the Patriot Act amended FISA to allow surveillance and physical searches so long as a "significant purpose" was to gather foreign intelligence[11]—no longer the primary purpose. This, for the first time, allowed the government to obtain surveillance and search orders even if the government's primary purpose was to gather evidence of domestic criminal activity. In other words, it is enough that the government may learn something about foreign related activities. The Patriot Act significantly extended the period the warrants are good for, included physical searches (section 207), and allowed the information gathered to be used for prosecution purposes whereas before it was strictly forbidden.[12] Judicial oversight is virtually nonexistent, as the FISC rejected no surveillance applications out of the nearly 15,000 submitted between 1979 and 2002. Another 20,000 or so were submitted between 2003 and 2013 alone, only 12 of which were ultimately rejected.[13] That is less than 0.06%.

After 2002, the Department of Justice sought approval of its new procedures which allowed the FBI to utilize FISA even when its primary purpose was domestic law enforcement. In a startling unanimous opinion, the FISC acknowledged that government agents applying for warrants had misrepresented facts and ruled that government procedures aimed at sidestepping the Fourth Amendment were improper.[14] The opinion marked the first time that the FISA court made a public opinion. Not happy, the government appealed to the FISC of Review, which was the first and only opportunity for this curious court to hear a case. Like the FISC, the rules only allowed the government to appear before it and the hearings were conducted in secret. The court ruled in the government favor and overturned the decision, and because the government is the only party that can appeal, it naturally was satisfied with the opinion.[15]

The secret wiretaps approved and used to spy on Brandon Mayfield, his home, and law office were originally intended for use only by FBI agents conducting open-ended "intelligence" gathering activities, and not for use in criminal trials. However, they were used by the FBI as an opportunity to sift through virtually every one of Brandon's "papers and effects" in order to build a case against him. (He would learn later that the material witness search and arrest warrants were used to do the same). The original FISA warrant application had to assert that Mr. Mayfield was a foreign power or an agent of a foreign power. The FBI's original access to Brandon's home therefore originated in the entirely false and unsubstantiated claim that he was an al-Qaeda member or affiliate.

Had Brandon been provided a copy of the application, he could have shown the oath or affirmation to be false or perjured. The problem with secret searches though is that, by the nature of their secrecy, one generally does not know when he has been subject to them, and thus can rarely challenge them. But for an unusual turn of events, Brandon Mayfield never would have learned that a secret warrant from a secret court—America's Star Chamber—was ever authorized.

§ § §

[1] Detroit Free Press v. Ashcroft, 303 F.3d 681, 683 (2002).

[2] Simkin, John. "John Lilburne." Spartacus Educational. Web. 25 Sept. 2014. <http://spartacus-educational.com/STUlilburne.htm>.

[3] Pyle, Christopher. "The Right to Remain Silent in an Age of Mass Surveillance." *Counterpunch.* 22 Aug. 2013. Web. 14. Mar. 2015. <http://www.counterpunch.org/2013/08/22/the-right-to-remain-silent-in-an-age-of-mass-surveillance>

[4] *Id.*

[5] *See* supra note 2.

[6] Schmidt, Steffen W., Mack C. Shelley, Barbara A. Bardes, Lynne E. Ford, William E. Maxwell, Ernest Crain, and Adolfo Santos. "Chapter 15." American government and politics today. Boston, MA: Suzanne Jean, 2012. 525. Print.

[7] Constitutional Access to Justice Provisions - Judicial Administration State Links | NCSC.org." National Center For State Courts. Web. 25 Sept. 2014. < http://www.ncsc.org/Topics/Judicial-Officers/Judicial-Administration/State-Links.aspx?cat=Constitutional%20Access%20to%20Justice%20Provisions#Oregon>

[8] Katz v. United States, 389 U.S. 347 (1967).

[9] See United States v. U.S. District Court, 407 U.S. 297 (1972), also known as the Keith Case.

[10] Poe, M. K.. "Author Notes." Silicon seduction. S.l.: Iuniverse Inc., 2011. 368. Print.

[11] Uniting and Strengthening America by Providing Appropriate Tools Required to Intercept and Obstruct Terrorism Act of 2001, Pub. L. No. 107-56, 115 Stat. 272, § 218 (2001) (enacted Oct. 26, 2001).

[12] *Id.* at § 207. In July 2003, Senators Lisa Murkowski and Ron Wyden introduced a bill entitled Protecting the Rights of Individuals Act that would provide, among other things, that sneak-and-peek authority only be available in the limited number of cases (such as risk of flight, destruction of evidence etc.) and that "a significant purpose" be replaced with "the primary purpose." The bill has been read twice in the Senate and referred to the Committee on the Judiciary where it has apparently died.

[13] "Foreign Intelligence Surveillance Act Court Orders 1979-2014." EPIC. Web. 25 Sept. 2014. <http://epic.org/privacy/wiretap/stats/ fisa_stats.html>

[14] *See* In re All Matters Submitted to the Foreign Intelligence Surveillance Court, 218 F. Supp. 2d 611(U.S. Foreign Intell. Surveil. Ct. 2002).

[15] *See* In re: Sealed Case No. 02-001, 310 F.3d 717 (2002).

Chapter 5
Sneaky Little Devils

"The Right of the People to be secure in their persons, houses, papers and effects against unreasonable searches and seizures, shall not be violated, and no warrants shall issue, but upon probable cause, supported by oath or affirmation, and particularly describing the place to be searched, and the persons or things to be seized."
Fourth Amendment of the U.S. Constitution.

On April 8, 2004, Mona dropped Shane off at school and proceeded with her daily errands. Between approximately 11:00 AM and 1:00 PM, she went to "Ross Dress for Less" to return some clothes and then to a local halal meat market to buy some groceries. Typically she would come to work after dropping off Shane, but she had decided to stay home after running her errands that day.

Upon returning home from shopping, Mona placed her grocery bags outside the entrance and fumbled through her keys to open the bottom lock of the door (not the bolt). She heard a click and naturally tried to turn the doorknob, but the door did not budge—the bolt had been locked. No one in the family ever locked the top bolt. Usually the last person to leave the house would twist the lock of the doorknob while still inside and then slam the door shut once outside. Mona's first thought was that Brandon had come home for lunch, which was rare, and that he had locked the top bolt, which was implausible. She immediately called him on her cell phone. "Brandon, did you come home for lunch today?"

"No, I have been here at the office all day."

"Are you sure?" she insisted.

"Yes, I'm sure. Why? What's wrong?" he answered, unamused.

"Well I just got home and find it very unusual that the deadbolt was locked when I did not lock it," Mona said with trepidation in her voice.

"Mona, you must have bolted it and just forgot. I'm sure you just forgot."

"No, I did not forget," she retorted.

"Ok sweetie, I don't know what to tell you. I have work I need to do. All I can say is you must have forgotten."

Once inside, Mona laid down her groceries quietly and scanned the place for any abnormalities. As she did so, she was overcome with an eerie feeling that someone else was in the house besides her. Gripped with fear, she began to call out to her black and white tuxedo cat. "Pooty! Here kitty, kitty! Pooty!" When he came to her, the obedient and loyal cat that he was, she wished he could talk. She looked into his eyes in hopes that his dumb expression could divulge some secret. Nothing. He seemed unfazed. She wanted to ask him what he had seen—if someone had intruded into their home. There was no other explanation for the deadbolt being locked. Rather comically to anyone but someone who has been in such a situation, she talked to him. The only eyes that might have seen anything were restricted by a mouth that could not communicate. And so he listened, silent.

Mona then walked over to Shane's room, located above the garage, but froze with her toes pushed against the bottom footstep. It was the creepiest part of the house, colder and more remote from the rest. She looked up, horrified by what, or who, she might find. What if someone was up there? A ghost? A Jinn? She decided that if something was indeed hiding in there, she did not want to confront it. Mona closed the door and prayed to God it was all in her head.

When Brandon came home, he fruitlessly inspected the door for any malfunctions and questioned Mona. "Are you sure there is no chance that you left the door bolted and forgot?" he asked.

"No, I told you I did not forget. Brandon, I am scared. I felt something in the house."

"What do you mean *something*?"

"I mean—I felt as if there was someone or something in this house when I came home, maybe a Jinn. I don't know, something was in this house."

"You mean a Jinn, like a genie? The devil?" Brandon was less superstitious and was incredulous of paranormal activity in the house. He accepted that Jinns existed in some form alongside man, the most infamous being "Shaytan" (or Satan, the devil), but he never thought one would be in his house. It was strange enough that people ever saw them and Brandon, more rational, attributed strange eerie feelings to intuition or emotion.

"Brandon, I don't know. I'm just telling you what I felt. Something evil was in here."

Brandon assured her everything was alright and insisted they end the conversation. Inside though, he was worried, particularly because Mona had such a good memory. He was scared too, not that it was a Jinn but a different kind of devil, in flesh and blood.

§ § §

Such fear was compounded when a similar incident happened again the following week on April 13th. Mona and Brandon were at work all day. Mona arrived before Brandon, and when he got to the office she reprimanded him.

"Why did you not lock the door when you left yesterday?" she interrogated him.

"I *did*. What are you talking about?"

"No you did not. The little button on the knob on the inside had popped out. You did not push it in completely," she insisted.

"Well I don't know what you're talking about, because I always lock the door before I leave and I locked it yesterday."

Brandon thought nothing of her comment and continued working. Mona left before he did and was the first to arrive home with the kids after she had picked them up. Again the deadbolt was unexplainably locked. Mona gave the key to Shane to verify that it was bolted. She did not want to be told again it was her imagination.

"Shane, tell me I'm not crazy and that the bolt is bolted."

"You're right. It's locked. Maybe you locked it and forgot," he said.

Before anyone went in, she used her cell phone to call Brandon and handed to the phone to Shane. "Shane, tell your dad that the bolt is bolted."

"Dad, it's me Shane. Mom's right. The bolt is bolted."

"Okay Shane, I believe you. Let me talk to your mom." Brandon remembered that the youngest son Samir was the last one out of the house that morning and could not have bolted the lock because he had no key. At that point, Brandon and Mona knew somebody had been in their home.

"Mona, tell Shane and the kids to check everything in the house carefully to see if there are any signs of somebody being there or anything missing. Look for things moved, blinds opened, anything at all that looks out of place." When they went in, they immediately noticed the power had gone off and all the electronic appliances and clocks were flashing. Mona called Portland General Electric (PGE) and was met with no help.

"Ma'am you should try to check the breakers. Have you checked the breaker?" the operator most likely read from a script.

"Yes, I checked the breakers and they were not tripped, and if they have been they're turned back on. Do you know if there has been a power outage here?" Mona asked.

"No Ms. Mayfield. There has been no outage in your area," the operator answered.

"What about a scheduled work repair? Did you send somebody to check the meter or make a repair?"

"No ma'am. There hasn't been a power outage, scheduled visit, or repair. Sorry." Was he apologizing for her seeming lunacy? Mona did not know but felt she was not going to get any answers from a clueless man who was just doing his job.

"That's okay. Thanks for your assistance."

As Mona was talking on the phone, the kids were looking for signs of anything out of place. Shane noticed, upon close inspection, that there were footprints from large shoes pressed into his carpet, but none of the family wore shoes in the house. It was a strict policy that even guests leave their shoes at the door since cleanliness was next to godliness and Muslims took the adage seriously. Shane also noticed his blinds were cracked open at about five feet up, which was a foot higher than anyone else in the house would have cracked it to look out the window. When Brandon came home, he verified these things and personally concluded either the house had been burglarized or the FBI had been there. The latter seemed more plausible since no valuables or money had been stolen. Still, concerned about having important documents in the house after the break-in, Brandon invested in a safety deposit box to secure cash and other items such as passports (expired at the time) and birth certificates. It was his first defense against the mysterious intruders.

§ § §

Section 213 of the Patriot Act, the "sneak and peek" provision, allows the government to secretly search and seize property that constitutes evidence of a U.S. criminal offense without immediately notifying the owner.[1] This was made a permanent part of the act.[2] In 2003 a bill sponsored by Representatives Butch Otter, Dennis Kucinich, and Ron Paul (among others) to end funding for the sneak and peak provisions passed the House but failed to pass the Senate.[3]

Some of the more controversial sections were set to expire but are repeatedly extended, including sections 203 (allowing evidence acquired without a warrant to be used for criminal purposes), 206 (regarding roving wiretaps), 218 (permitting a probable cause exception for wiretaps and searches), and 215 (compelling businesses and libraries to produce personal records).[4]

Many of the Patriot Act's provisions were to sunset beginning December 31, 2005, approximately four years after its passage. However, even in the face of its critics, in July of 2005 the U.S. Senate passed a reauthorization bill with substantial changes to several sections of the Act, while the House reauthorization bill kept most of the Act's original language.[5] The two bills were then reconciled in a conference committee that was criticized by Senators from both the Republican and Democratic parties for ignoring civil liberty concerns.[6]

The bill, which removed most of the changes from the Senate version, passed Congress on March 2, 2006, and was signed into law by President George W. Bush on March 9 and 10, 2006.[7] On May 26, 2011, President Barack Obama signed another four-year extension of most of the key provisions in the Patriot Act.[8]

§ § §

[1] Uniting and Strengthening America by Providing Appropriate Tools Required to Intercept and Obstruct Terrorism Act of 2001 [hereinafter USA PATRIOT Act], Pub. L. No. 107-56, 115 Stat. 272, § 213 (enacted Oct. 26, 2001).

[2] Lichtblau, Eric. "Senate Makes Permanent Nearly All Provisions of Patriot Act, With a Few Restrictions." *The New York Times*. The New York Times, 29 July 2005. Web. 29 Aug. 2014. <http://www.nytimes.com/2005/07/30/politics/30patriot.html?pagewanted=all&_r=0-Senate>.

[3] LibertyThink. "'Security and Freedom Ensured Act of 2003' or the SAFE Act." *American Patriot Friends Netowrk*. 21 Oct. 2003. Web. 29 Aug. 2014. <http://www.apfn.net/messageboard/10-22-03/discussion.cgi.52.html>.

[4] The Stream Team. "Timeline: A history of the Patriot Act | Al Jazeera America." *Al Jazeera America*. 23 Oct. 2013. Web. 29 Aug. 2014. <http://america.aljazeera.com/watch/shows/the-stream/the-stream-officialblog/2013/10/23/timeline-a-historyofthepatriotact.html>.

[5] *Id.*

[6] *Id.*

[7] *Id.*

[8] *Id.*

Chapter 6
Client Unconfidentiality

"Just because you're paranoid doesn't mean they aren't after you." Joseph Heller, *Catch 22*.

What was mild suspicion soon became full-fledged paranoia after one particularly terrifying incident left the entire family in fear of its privacy. On an April day Shane woke up sick. As was usual, Mona called his school and let them know he would not be attending. She then left him home alone to go to work.

Shane lay in bed till around noon before getting up to grab something to eat in the kitchen downstairs. As he walked from the kitchen to the living room with his food, he spied a Hispanic male of medium build carrying a white envelope through the living room window. He figured it must have been some sort of mailman or solicitor. Shane watched as the man approached the entrance door and disappeared out of his line of vision. But there was no knock. Instead he heard the doorknob jiggle as if someone was trying to break in. Panicking and convinced the house was being burglarized, he pulled the cordless phone off the stand and ran upstairs to Sharia's room and crawled inside the adjacent attic. It was dusty and dark, with heaping boxes of toys, photo albums, and other memorabilia. As he was attempting to dial his mom for the second time, the phone began to ring, sending a bolt of dread through his body. Scared of who it could be, but relieved he would no longer be alone, he answered.

It was his aunt Naveen calling to talk to Mona. Shane struggled to catch his breath and then confided in a whisper, "Naveen, somebody is trying to break into the house."

"Shane, are you sure?" Naveen asked.

"Yes, Naveen. I saw them go to the door and they tried to open it, so I ran to the attic."

"Do you think they know you're there?"

Shane hesitated. "Naveen, I don't know. I don't think so but I'm worried. Mom isn't picking up her phone."

"Okay Shane, just be calm. I want you to hang up and call your Mom again." Shane tried reaching his mother but to no avail. Meanwhile, Naveen dialed Mona and got an answer just as Mona was leaving the office to run an errand.

"Mona, what the hell is going on?"

"What, what are you talking about?" Mona said, oblivious.

"I just called Shane and he is scared out of his wits. He said someone is trying to break into the house. He has been trying to call you but you never pick up."

"That's weird. My phone never rang. Are you sure?"

"Yes Mona. I just about called the Portland police myself. You need to call and find out what's going on."

"Okay, well, let me go. I'm going to call him right now. Bye." Mona fumbled with her cellphone as she punched in the digits while trying to watch the road.

Shane was waiting for his mother to call, his finger trembling on the answer button as if it was a trigger. Just as soon as the phone began to ring he pressed down.

"Shane, what's going on?" His mother yelled.

"Mom?!" He blurted. "Mom, somebody tried to break into the house."

"What? Speak up! I can't hear you. Why are you whispering?" Mona asked.

"I said somebody tried to break in," he repeated more loudly and slowly.

"Where are you?" Mona asked, still incredulous.

"I'm hiding in the attic in Sharia's room. I saw someone come to the door and start trying to come into the house."

"How do you know it's not a neighbor or someone looking for an address or the mailman?" she asked, masking her growing fear. The thought that her son was in harm's way chilled her to the bones, and yet she could not believe that anyone would break into the house.

"Mom, why wouldn't they try and knock on the door and just start fiddling with the lock and come in?" Shane muttered under his breath.

"Yeah, you're right. It is kind of weird." She paused. "Anyway, stay on the phone and don't move. I am in the car and I'm coming straight home."

"Okay. When you get close, drive around the house first and see if anyone is parked outside."

Shane hung up the phone and wedged himself behind a box of old junk. It was the longest fifteen minutes he had ever experienced, spent in total darkness. In any other situation he would have wanted to be a man, but curled up in the attic, knees to his chest, he could feel the pounding heart of a scared boy. The silence scared him the most, because he knew it could be broken at any moment. The door could be smashed down and that man, whom he could barely recreate in his mind, could point a gun right at him.

When Mona reached home, whoever had been there was gone. Mona immediately ran to the attic and yelled to Shane that it was safe to come out. He trembled out of the door and recounted all he had seen. After hearing all the facts, Mona called Brandon to update him of what had happened.

As was the case before, Brandon and Mona wondered if the electric or gas company could have sent an employee to read the meter. Mona called them and asked when they made scheduled visits. Both companies verified that no visits took place that day. More disconcertingly, there had been some recent arsons in the neighborhood that the family thought may have been connected to the man Shane saw. By Saturday, after much brooding, Brandon decided to call the police to report the incident. The 911 operator said the report was not an emergency and for Brandon to talk to a detective at the Beaverton or Hillsboro police department. Brandon called the number and gave what information he could and inquired if they had any leads on the arson incident. They said he would have to call back on a weekday but Brandon never did.

§ § §

Mona usually arrived at the law office shortly before Brandon did. One day in April, 2004, she got to work and tried to turn on both of the computers, but only Brandon's started up. She was upset and blamed him for shutting down her computer improperly. She insisted that it was his fault. Everything was his fault those days: the locked deadbolt, the broken computer, probably the power outage. The mysterious occurrences were starting to frustrate Brandon, who had no other explanation for them.

"Yesterday my computer was working. You were the last one out of the office, so what did you do?" Mona accused him, reasonably justified. Brandon was technologically challenged and the most likely culprit of the computer problem.

"I did not do anything. I shut it down like I always do." Every time she tried to boot it up it would prompt a "systems error" screen. Puzzled, Brandon decided to have Shane, who was more computer savvy, come look at it.

Shane opened the computer and examined the hardware. At just 15, he knew enough to know something was amiss. "Dad, it looks like somebody removed the connector from the hard drive and did not secure it again properly. This old computer is configured so that if you unplug the connector from the hard drive and don't plug it in properly before turning it on it will fry the hard drive and delete your entire system."

It was at that exact moment that Brandon suspected someone had been in his office, and it was most likely not a robber. Brandon brought the computer home and Shane labored on it over the weekend. He put in another hard drive and connector from an old computer in his bedroom and returned the old computer to work. It took Brandon and Mona most of the week to get it networked properly again and download all the programs files and sites they used in their practice. Consequently, business was set back considerably because of the malfunction. Whoever the intruders were, they were sloppy menaces whom Brandon was growing increasingly impatient and irritated with.

§ § §

There was also a suspicious car frequently parked in front of the law office that Brandon had not seen before. Brandon noticed it among the others because it had a military sticker from PANG Air Force base with a star on it. He wondered if it indicated rank, and why the car was regularly parked near his small office complex. After seeing it around from time to time he checked online to see if there was anything telling about the base, such as where it was and what units were there. There were only a couple of articles on it, describing the PANG Air Force base as the home of a new special operations unit, a sort of pseudo-military/civilian unit. It was apparently an air reserve unit in Portland.

One Friday, as Brandon left to go to the Mosque for the noon prayer, he watched in his rear view mirror as the car pulled out behind him. Its driver was an older, heavy-set white man in his late 50's or early 60's. Instead of turning right toward the mosque that day, Brandon took a left to see if the man would follow. It may have been coincidental, but the mysterious man trailed behind.

Later that night, Brandon confided to Mona that they might be watched, even in their own living room, kitchen, and bedrooms. Brandon began to refrain from openly making politically charged comments. If he talked politics on the phone with friends or relatives he always joked that someone could be listening, half-believing it to be true.

As time went on he became even more convinced that Mona and he were being followed and listened to. One afternoon, after much rumination, he asked Mona to step outside with him.

"Mona, listen carefully to me."

"Why are you whispering?" She looked at Brandon.

"Just listen. If...if we were to be falsely arrested for anything, we need to have a plan for what to do with the kids and decide where they should go, alright?" For the first time in his life, Brandon felt completely helpless and in the dark. He had surmised that his family was being watched and concluded that the only explanation was that he or Mona were somehow suspected of "criminal activity" or else targets of a crime. Brandon was an uninhibited personality, unafraid to speak his opinions about the government's mishaps or about the Patriot Act and unlawful wars. But he knew he needed to keep his mouth shut for the safety of his family, especially his children. As he contemplated his possible wrongful arrest, the kids were his first concern.

"Alright, I agree. I think we should call either Naveen or your mom if anything happens." Mona answered.

"Yeah. I'll call my Mom." Shortly thereafter, Brandon called his mom in Kansas. "Mom, Mona and I have been talking and are concerned. If anything were to happen to us we want you to take care of the kids, if necessary." It was a rather strange and unexpected conversation. Brandon's mom, Avnell, was not quite sure of the purpose or urgency in his sudden request and asked what prompted him.

"Look, mom. If we were to somehow suddenly disappear, perhaps fall out of the sky in a plane accident, or if agents of the government secretly sweep in and arrest us, like Captain Yee,[1] I would like your assurance that you could come to Portland on the first flight and take the kids back to Kansas with you." She promised Brandon she would and tried to convince him he had nothing to worry about. But perhaps she was wrong.

Brandon could not explain the impending doom he felt at the prospect of his phones being tapped and his home and office searched. He knew something bad was happening, but could have never fathomed what was transpiring in secret.

§ § §

Muslims are a targeted community under siege for the failure of the U.S. government to prevent the attacks by foreign extremists on September 11, 2001. Fifteen of the nineteen hijackers were Saudi citizens, three from the UAE, and one from Egypt. All were affiliated with al-Qaeda. The U.S. had already extradited and convicted Ramsi Yousef, one of the main perpetrators of the first World Trade Center attack in 1996, for his inflight bombing in 1993 of a 747 bound from Manila to Tokyo,[2] which was done as a trial run for later attacks on American flights. The FAA had reports that Osama Bin Laden had discussed hijacking a U.S. air carrier in an effort to free the blind Egyptian Cleric Abdul Rahman as early as 1999. In 2011, it was discovered that the FBI had withheld from the 9/11 commission information it had obtained about at least 11 of the hijackers, including Mohamad Atta, in connection with a Sarasota Florida home two weeks before the attacks.[3]

In 2011 it also came to light that the NYPD, with funding from the White House and help from the CIA, had long been engaged in ethnic mapping by use of Muslim mosque-rakers and mosque-crawlers, blurring the line between foreign and domestic spying.[4] Plain clothes Arab officers called rakers would go into Muslim neighborhoods, raking the coals for hot spots—meaning they would take pictures of mosques and Muslim neighbor-hoods, cafes, hookah bars, write down ethnic names and details, and put this information into police reports. The goal was to build profiles of where

Muslims ate, shopped, prayed, watched sports, and what internet cafes they went to, bringing in a vast amount of information about American Muslims.

In addition to rakers, they also used undercover officers as crawlers—informants utilized as listening posts inside the mosques reporting back on things such as what the imam is saying at Friday prayer, announcements to participate in nonviolent protests, or encouragement to write local politicians.[5]

None of these spying activities were motivated by any suspicion of any particular crime. Of all the data collected, there was only one documented actual crime (a store thought to have sold a counterfeit DVD).[6] It is estimated that the Bush and Obama administrations have provided $135 million to the New York and New Jersey region through the High Intensity Drug Trafficking Area program, known as HIDTA, which helped fund this spying on Muslim neighborhoods,[7] which is contrary to the administration's stated purpose of outreach to American Muslims and their comments that law enforcement should not put entire communities under suspicion.[8]

In 2007, the NYPD released a ninety-two page report titled "Radicalization in the West," warning that impressionable Muslim-American men are being primed for jihad at such "radicalization incubators" as "cafes, cab driver hangouts, flophouses, prisons, student associations, nongovernmental organizations, hookah (water pipe) bars, butcher shops, and book stores." [9] The study warned that while in the first stage these men "look, act, talk, and walk like everyone around them," they are in fact "slowly building the mind-set, intention and commitment to conduct jihad." The report even mentioned white water rafting as an activity to watch for.[10]

There are widespread and countless examples of Islamophobia in the training of local, state, and national law enforcement personnel. Trainers for American law enforcement and military personnel have included "experts" such as Robert Spencer, co-founder of *Stop the Islamization of America* (SIOA), and "former terrorist" (whatever that means) Walid Shoebat. Coincidently, SIOA has been designated a hate group by the Southern Poverty Law Center, and CNN aired a two-part series exposing Shoebat as an anti-Islam fraud.[11]

The Department of Homeland Security (DHS), which provides most of the Federal funding for state and local training, recently issued a set of recommendations for countering prejudiced training.[12] In 2012, as a result of calls from Muslim advocacy groups for an investigation into training materials, the Federal Bureau of Investigation revealed around 1,000 documents that an internal probe has described as inappropriate.[13]

Many in the Muslim community feel a sense of betrayal when for years law enforcement officials have been approaching the American Muslim community, encouraging open dialogue and positive engagement. The FBI, the JTTFs (Joint Terrorism Task Forces), and NYPD are chasing imaginary or expected leads based on religion. It is a clear example of ethnic, religious, and racial profiling funded by the U.S. government.

When Timothy McVeigh bombed the federal building in Oklahoma we did not call him a fundamental Christian terrorist. We did not set out to question and interrogate every Christian or to monitor and infiltrate every church from Miami to Portland. But when Muslim criminals brought down the World Trade Center we did.

§ § §

[1] Captain Yee, a Muslim chaplain and West Point graduate was arrested as he headed back from Guantanamo for a brief planned visit with his family in the U.S. He was charged with espionage, spying, aiding the enemy, and sedition, and his attorneys were told that he could face execution. He spent a total of 76 days in solitary confinement only ultimately to be released and all charges dropped. Brandon had not met Yee but knew of him having led the same Patriot missile platoon as Yee in Bitburg Germany, after Yee left to become an Army chaplain.

[2] Jenkins, Brian, and Reuters. "Plane terror suspects convicted on all counts."*CNN.* Cable News Network, 5 Sept. 1996. Web. 31 Aug. 2014. <http://www.cnn.com/US/9609/05/terror.plot/index.html>

[3] Summers, Anthony , and Dan Christensen. "FBI found direct ties between 9/11 hijackers and Saudis living in Florida; Congress kept in dark. "Broward Bulldog. 8 Sept. 2011. Web. 31 Aug. 2014. <http://www.browardbulldog.org/2011/09/fbi-found-direct-ties-between-911-hijackers-and-saudis-living-in-florida-congress-kept-in-dark>.

[4] Apuzzo, Matt , and Adam Goldman. "With CIA help, NYPD moves covertly in Muslim areas." AP. 23 Aug. 2011. Web. 31 Aug. 2014. <http://

www.ap.org/Content/AP-in-the-News/2011/With-CIA-help-NYPD-moves-covertly-in-Muslim-areas>.

[5] *Id.*

[6] *Id.*

[7] Sullivan, Eileen. "White House helps pay for NYPD Muslim surveillance." AP. 27 Feb. 2012. Web. 31 Aug. 2014. <http://www.ap.org/content/ap-in-the-news/2012/white-house-helps-pay-for-nypd-muslim-surveillance>.

[8] "White House helps pay for New York Police Department surveillance of Muslims: report ." NY Daily News. 27 Feb. 2012. Web. 31 Aug. 2014. <http://www.nydailynews.com/new-york/white-house-helps-pay-nypd-surveillance-muslims-report-article-1.1029173>.

[9] Silber, Mitchell, and Arvin Bhatt. "Radicalization in the West: The Homegrown Threat." The New York City Police Department. 2007. 31 Aug. 2014. <http://www.nyc.gov/html/nypd/downloads/pdf/public_information/NYPD_Report-Radicalization_in_the_West.pdf>

[10] *Id.*

[11] "Video: Anderson Cooper Exposes 'Ex-Terrorist' Walid Shoebat as Fraud (CAIR)." YouTube. CNN, 14 July 2011. Web. 31 Aug. 2014. <http://www.youtube.com/watch?v=pJN00dBhZVk>.

[12] See Countering Violent Extremism (CVE) Training Guidance and Best Practices.

[13] "FBI internal documents reveal anti-Muslim bias." PressTV. 17 Feb. 2012. Web. 31 Aug. 2014. <http://edition.presstv.ir/detail/227188.html>

Chapter 7
Tell it to the Judge

"Collective fear stimulates herd instinct, and tends to produce ferocity toward those who are not regarded as members of the herd." Bertrand Russell, *Unpopular Essays*

The old ROTC building at Portland State University where Brandon once trained as a cadet passed in a blur as he and the FBI agents arrived at the rear of the federal courthouse where U.S. marshals were waiting. At every step of the way, the marshals were there to usher the alleged criminal around. One of them called out something on his hand microphone and then motioned for two others to unbolt and open the steel doors leading to a parking garage. Brandon heard this from inside the SUV, their voices partially muted through the car's window. The sunlight abruptly turned to darkness as the vehicle passed into a large, empty, concrete structure.

The gates closed behind them and a female marshal approached Brandon's passenger window, asking him to step out of the vehicle. The agent seated next to Brandon handed Brandon the affidavit and a thin stack of papers in what must have been a final act of pity or contrition. A "goodbye and good luck" gesture it seemed. Brandon clutched to them graciously and exchanged a silent thank you to him, a quick nod of the head. Still bewildered, he then stepped out from the SUV. "Face the vehicle," the marshal demanded as she proceeded to frisk him.

During the process, the woman placed a set of heavy leg chains around his ankles, and a bolt of anxiety ran through Brandon. How was he going to walk in them? "Turn around and put your hands out in front you," she commanded. As he turned slowly, she put her chest to his back and secured belly chains around his mid-section, looping them through his handcuffs. It was the crowning disgrace of the arrest, and now he was completely unable to move normally. When she finished, she told him to walk toward the building's entrance.

Such a task was infinitely more difficult when shackled and chained. Brandon shuffled one foot at a time, taking small, intentional steps so as not to trip. The chains jangled violently in asynchrony and echoed in the spacious parking garage as he waddled on. A couple of the marshals escorted him through the thick double doors, past a small processing area, and then through a short maze of halls to several empty holding cells.

"You'll be held here for now." A marshal pointed to one of the cells. Brandon stared vacantly through the metal bars and then back at the marshal. He did not want to go in. Naturally. No man would willingly escort himself into a cage—especially an innocent man. Brandon was pained as he stepped over the boundary from the free side to the criminal side.

"I'd like to speak with a lawyer, Tom Nelson. Can I speak with him?" Tom Nelson was an attorney whom Brandon had only communicated with over phone and email but had never actually met. The marshal said he would make sure Tom was contacted, but Brandon was not sure what he meant by that. Would he come back and let him make a phone call? Or would he contact Tom directly?

The marshal slammed the gate shut in Brandon's face and left in a rather nonchalant mood. It was just business, impersonal business, and that bothered Brandon. Did the marshal see a hardened criminal when he saw the chained and shackled man helpless in front of him? Did he entertain the idea that whatever it was, maybe the man in the cell hadn't done it? Brandon mused over this, over all the bystanders and officers who had seen him paraded about, and a deep shame set in. He agonized, fingers linked on the bars for a couple seconds, before turning to his new fate.

The holding cell was approximately 10 to 12 feet long and 6 feet wide. It was clean and claustrophobic with a plastic bench, a toilet, and a small sink. Dim lights shined through the bars, and the cell resonated anytime a door was opened or closed in the hallway. He was not sure how long he would have to wait before someone came back, so he decided to finally take a look at the papers he had in hand. Sitting on the cold plastic bench, he read in detail—for the first time—the affidavit in support of his arrest.

§ § §

Publisher's note: The below text from the affidavit has been truncated. The formatting and text have been slightly modified for purposes of brevity.

AFFIDAVIT [1]

I, Richard Werder, being first duly sworn, depose and state that:

1. I am a sworn federal law enforcement officer employed by the Department of Justice, Federal Bureau of Investigation FBI, and have been so employed since 1983. I am currently assigned as an investigator working International Terrorism matters in conjunction with the FBI Joint Terrorism Task Force (JTTF), Portland Oregon...

2. This affidavit is submitted in support of a warrant for arrest of material witness **BRANDON BIERI MAYFIELD**...

3. ...Since this affidavit is being submitted in support of an application for a warrant to arrest a material witness, I have...set forth only the facts that I believe are necessary to establish the necessary probable cause.

SUMMARY OF INVESTIGATION

4. On March 11, 2004, at approximately 7:39 a.m. (Madrid Time) the first of a series of 10 explosions at four sites occurred on commuter trains... in Madrid, Spain. The death toll...has been reported at approximately 200 individuals with more than 1500 injured, including three United States' citizens.

5. [A Renault Kangoo van] was found in the vicinity [of the Alcala de Henares station]. Eyewitnesses...observed three individuals handling some backpacks next to the van [before the attack].

6. During a search of the van, the SNP recovered a blue plastic bag underneath the passenger seat [within which were] several detonators and remnants of explosives.

7. On March 17, 2004, the SNP provided the FBI with photographic images of the latent fingerprints that were recovered from the plastic bag containing

the detonators that was found in the Kangoo van, including Latent Finger Print #17 (hereinafter LFP#17). All the fingerprints were provided to the Latent Print Unit at the FBI Laboratory in Quantico, Virginia. Senior Fingerprint Examiner [name removed], submitted LFP#17 into the Automated Fingerprint Identification System (AFIS) for a possible matches. **BRANDON BIERI MAYFIELD** was identified as a potential match to the unknown print...[He] then requested and received two known fingerprint cards of Mayfield. The first card [was] obtained in connection with a criminal arrest for burglary...on December 22, 1984. The second [was from] his service in the United States Army...[He] identified in excess of 15 points of identification during his comparison and has advised that he considers the match to be a 100% identification of **BRANDON BIERI MAYFIELD.** The 100% identification was verified by Supervisory Fingerprint Specialist...Wieners...[and retired FBI fingerprint examiner Massey].

8. In mid-April it became apparent that the preliminary findings of the Forensic Science Division of the SNP...were not consistent with those of the FBI laboratory. As a result, a meeting was held between a representative of the FBI's Latent Fingerprint Unit and approximately ten members of the Forensic Science Division of the SNP...Before the meeting SNP personnel indicated that...a final determination had not been rendered. [The FBI believed the SNP were then satisfied with the identification and the FBI stands by the 100% positive identification].

BACKGROUND OF IDENTIFIED SUBJECT

11. ...**MAYFIELD** works as an attorney [and is] married to Mona Mayfield, aka Mona Mohamed, and a check through the Bureau of Immigration and Customs Enforcement (BICE) showed that **Mona Mayfield** was born in Egypt...

12. [Mayfield] first entered active duty military service as an enlisted soldier in the United States Army on July 31, 1985...**MAYFIELD** was commissioned as a Second Lieutenant on August 17, 1992, through the ROTC program at Portland State University. He re-entered active duty...and was honorably discharged from active duty on May 18, 1994. His medical discharge was due to a shoulder injury.

13. [In] October 2002 **BRANDON MAYFIELD** represented Jeffrey Leon Battle in a civil case involving the custody of Battle's minor child. Battle was arrested on October, 2002 on federal terrorism charges of Conspiracy to Levy War Against the United States...to Provide Material Support and Resources to Al-Qaida and the Taliban...[The subsequent paragraphs discuss in great detail the terrorist charges and allegations brought against Battle, a Muslim involved in the Portland Seven case.]

15. Records obtained from Verizon indicate...a telephonic contact between [Mayfied's home phone and the phone number subscribed to by Pete Seda]...

16. [Pete] is the Director of the Al-Haramain Islamic Foundation (AHIF) in Ashland, Oregon. [The affidavit goes on to discuss Pete's "terrorist" connections and a criminal investigation into his dealings with the non-governmental organization AHIF. Official terrorist charges were brought against Pete and officially dropped after no evidence was found connecting him to terrorism. Affidavit mentions Pete's distributions of Qurans as indication of terroristic indoctrination, mentioning that there is an appendix in the Quran mandating jihad. The affidavit shows no sincere understanding of Arabic or the Quran and fails to acknowledge that jihad can mean any internal or external struggle in the name of God]...

19. Since March 21, 2004, surveillance agents have observed MAYFIELD drive to the Bilal Mosque...on several different occasions...

20. [Mayfield advertises his law office in a Muslim Yellow page directory, a publication in which General Electric and other major U.S. corporations advertise. The business link directory was administered by a corporation whose agent was linked to the secretary of Osama bin Laden. Somehow, the fact that Brandon was four degrees of separation away from Osama bin Laden was relevant in the affidavit, despite that everyone associated with GE would be equally tied to Osama bin Laden. An interesting report recently claimed that any two people in the world could be connected by 6 or fewer degrees of separation]...

21. [The affidavit concedes that records of travel indicate Brandon had not left the country in over a year, although more accurately he had not been on an international flight in over a decade. FBI alleges Brandon traveled under a fictitious name with false documents]...

24. I believe that based upon the likelihood of false travel documents in

existence, and the serious nature of the potential charges, **MAYFIELD** may attempt to flee the country if served with a subpoena...
25. Therefore, [I request] the issuance of a warrant for the arrest **BRANDON BIERI MAYFIELD...**

[Signed Richard Werder, May 6, 2004]

§ § §

Pete Seda (mentioned in the affidavit) was later cleared of all terrorist charges.[2] Neither Mona nor Brandon recalled having known Pete Seda prior to Brandon's arrest, nor his alleged terrorist affiliations. It may have been that Pete called the Mayfield's residence inquiring if Brandon practiced a certain type of law. While Freedom of Association is an activity protected by the First Amendment, it was used as yet another justification for the arrest. The NSA has since misinterpreted narrow Congressional grants of authority to allow for sweeping collection of phone records under Section 215 of the Patriot Act. Section 215 currently mandates that the government, prior to collection, have reasonable grounds to believe that the tangible things it seeks are "relevant to an authorized investigation."[3] The NSA has secretly interpreted the word "relevant" to be so expansive so as to be essentially meaningless: every phone record is relevant, in some tenuous way, to an investigation.

Moreover, the NSA uses such phone records for intelligence. Under alleged authority of Section 215, the government queries millions of phone calls to determine which phone numbers have been in contact, however minutely (or accidentally), with a suspected terrorist. While it is unknown if such technology was used to determine whether "Brandon" (i.e. anyone in his family who had used the shared landline) had made contact with Pete, the implications are clear: nearly everyone's records could fall into the government's hands. Originally, the government used a "three-hop" system, but this has been recently changed to a two-hop system upon the suggestion of the President[4] to identify potential "terrorists."

Former NSA Deputy Director John Inglis, who testified before the House Judiciary Committee, explained how the three-hop system works:

"When analysts think they have cause to suspect an individual, they will look at everyone that person has contacted, called the first hop away from the target. Then, in a series of exponential ripples, they look at everyone all those secondary people communicated with. And from that pool, they look at everyone those tertiary people contacted. This is called a second and a third hop." [5]

What the three-hop analysis meant was that, for every terrorist suspect, nearly one million people would fall within three degrees (hops) of a contact.[6] That implies that if the government were to identify a mere three hundred suspects (called "seeds"), it could potentially collect the phone metadata of every single adult American. While the legal basis for the government's alleged authority is complex, it boils down to the simple assertion that one does not have a reasonable expectation of privacy with regards to telephone records. According to the courts, information about who we contact over the phone is "voluntarily disclosed" to members of the public (i.e. the phone company), and thus no longer private. Accordingly, Fourth Amendment protections do not apply. Luckily, courts are seeing a shift in this outdated logic. Many senators, including senators Wyden, Heinrich, Paul, Lee, Durbin, Franken, and Leahy, among others, have pushed for efforts to restrict the bulk collection of Americans' phone records.[7] The former three of these senators expanded on their main objection to phone metadata collection in a jointly-authored *New York Times* op-ed published in November of 2013:

"The usefulness of the bulk collection program has been greatly ex-aggerated. We have yet to see any proof that it provides real, unique value in protecting national security. In spite of our repeated requests, the N.S.A. has not provided evidence of any instance when the agency used this program to review phone records that could not have been obtained using a regular court order or emergency authorization." [8]

§ § §

Still shackled and confined, Brandon lay down on the plastic bench, tried to position the leg constraints from cutting too deep into his ankles, and waited for something to happen. He held the affidavit with a death-grip and read it over and over until each line was seared into his memory. *So, this is the document that secured my arrest,* he thought. He was seething at it, at every irrelevant line supposedly establishing probable cause. What did Battles' desire to fight in Afghanistan have to do with anything? Or Mona's country of origin? Or the fact that one guy from one company, affiliated with the Muslim directory Brandon advertised in, knew a guy who knew Osama bin Laden? And why the mention of his mosque attendance? None of those "facts" established probable cause to believe Brandon was involved in the Madrid attacks. Probable cause must be relevant to the crime. Unless being a Muslim, praying in the mosque, marrying an Egyptian, and posting in the same directory as someone who might know someone who knows a terrorist were crimes, the affidavit was wildly speculative and blatantly prejudicial.

Brandon stared down at the affidavit, angered and disturbed. He looked back at the 100 percent match as if it were a typo meant to be 10 percent or 1 percent. He knew his fingerprint was not the one on the blue bag and would contest the issue with the judge. But his expectation to be released immediately turned to a more leveled optimism as he weighed the allegations charged against him. Federal agents had sworn to the local district court judge that they were 100 percent certain they had found his fingerprint on a bag of detonators left outside a train station in Madrid, Spain, the site of the March 11th bombings. Brandon's heart raced. Somebody had set out to frame him. The only "real" evidence presented, buried in irrelevancies, was the "100% fingerprint match."

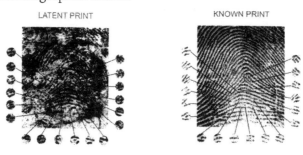

LATENT PRINT   KNOWN PRINT

Left: latent fingerprint. Right: Brandon's fingerprint.

After some indeterminate amount of time, a man approached his cell and asked Brandon to step out. "Mayfield, come on. You have someone here to visit you."

Anxiously, Brandon lowered his chained feet to the floor and waddled to the cell gate. The man grabbed the shoulder of Brandon's dress shirt as he clumsily stumbled into the hallway and headed to a secured visitation room.

When he reached the visitation room, though, no one was there. It was small with two round brushed aluminum seats firmly bolted to steel posts in the center of a concrete floor. There was a heavy steel entrance door on one side and a thick glass window enmeshed with screen on the other. A small, greasy black phone rested on the wall near the window, and the only connection to the outside world was a paper thin slot at the bottom of the window, big enough to pass a document but too thin to pass a pen. On the other side were carpet and two plush chairs for the attorneys or public defenders that came to see their clients. The irony set in as he realized what it must have been like for all his clients when he came to visit them. He was accustomed to the lawyer's side and—from comfortable seating—he would reassure them that everything would be okay. Now, he was the one boxed into the small room, and he knew that there would be no reassuring word to console him. The government had turned the tables on him at the stroke of Judge Jones' pen, and the alleged charges against him were far too dire. He waited there in silence for what seemed like hours until Tom arrived.

He was just as Brandon imagined him on the phone: not too tall, nor too short, with a trimmed white-gray beard, black-rimmed glasses, and a pleasant demeanor. Brandon also saw in Tom many of his own traits; they were both passionate spokespersons for civil liberties, Muslim converts, and motorcycle enthusiasts.

"Selam alaykem," peace be on you, he greeted Brandon with an unbefitting but much welcomed smile.

"Alaykem aselam," and unto you. Brandon smirked. "Isn't it ironic that over the years we have never managed to meet, and now we see each other for the first time under these circumstances?" Tom was an old acquaintance and Muslim attorney whom Brandon would occasionally call for legal advice but whom he never managed to meet for over a decade.

"There's always a time for firsts," he replied in a rustic, gravelly voice.

It was a comfort and pleasure to see him finally, and if anyone could help Brandon out it was him. "Tom, I know you don't practice criminal law, but could you please help me find a criminal defense attorney and tell me what your take is on this all?"

"Brandon, this morning I have been getting calls from lots of news sources, and your name's spreading all over the media," he confided.

"How is that? This is supposed to be a grand jury proceeding and a material witness matter. Aren't these matters supposed to be closed?"

"I don't know, but..."

"What are they saying about me?" He was curious.

"They are asking if I know anything about the Portland attorney who is being held in connection with the Madrid Spain bombing," Tom continued.

"What did you say?"

"I said I did not know any more than they did. Anyway, I got this here and wanted to go over it with you." He had a copy of the arrest warrant affidavit in his hand with scribbled notes written on it. Brandon perused the document, trying to decipher Tom's handwriting as Tom remarked about the breadth of Islamic innuendo.

"There's a lot about you being Muslim and whatnot. Your wife is Egyptian, you've been seen entering a mosque on several occasions, and you listed your legal services in an Islamic directory."

"What does that have to do with a bombing that occurred halfway around the world, unless the FBI is saying that being Muslim is circumstantial evidence that I'm a terrorist?"

"Exactly. They're building a case around you being Muslim. It'd be different if you were just another Joe Shmoe. Very different," he intimated.

"So, they're religiously profiling me?" Brandon asked, somewhat rhetorically, somewhat seriously.

"Well, of course, and the affidavit makes it damn clear, Brandon." They continued discussing the arrest and affidavit briefly before they were alerted by U.S. Marshals.

"Mayfield, you are wanted in the judge's courtroom on the tenth floor of the building. You'll have to come with us."

"Alright," he responded to them, turning to Tom. "I'll meet you in the courtroom."

§ § §

The prisoner elevator was a cell in and of itself: small, claustrophobic, and metal. Brandon was confined in the dark cage and guarded by marshals. In there he felt a sense of humility, of a full-circle sort of knowledge and understanding. Before, he had only known half of the courtroom experience: that of a privileged and comfortable lawyer whose only fate on the line was his own income. Now, his entire future and life were on the line and he was a defendant, no longer a defender.

Just outside the elevator was a small area where the marshals removed the chains on his stomach and legs. He felt a brief moment of respite being able to walk freely. The handcuffs stayed on and he was not allowed to enter from the back of the courtroom, as he had once done as an attorney, but was instead made to enter through a side door as a criminal. Walking into the room he saw a familiar sight, only from a different perspective: it was dimly lit by two large hanging lamps and sterile, with a layered, contoured ceiling and dark, modern cherry wood pews in the back. The courtroom had a heavy wood barrier, about 3 feet tall, separating the spectators from the counsel's table, and a sprawling elevated judge's bench that was majestically perched in the front. There were no windows of any kind. This, coupled with the acoustic tiles that absorbed all sound, gave the room a dark, chamber-like atmosphere.

Brandon was still in his dress shirt and pants, with noticeable sweat stains growing under his armpits. Tom, already there, helped himself to a seat at a nearby table. At the opposite table were three U.S. attorneys whose job it was to convince Judge Jones that Brandon Mayfield was connected to the Madrid Spain bombings and that he was a terrorist—or at least enough of one to be imprisoned without bail.

In the back of the courtroom was a small group of men and women in black suits, most with their arms folded and all proud of their latest catch. He recognized the two agents who had arrested him earlier and wondered what they were thinking. As he grabbed a seat next to Tom, a black-robed figure entered the room, presumably Judge Jones. He was well-groomed and reminded Brandon of a dad from one of those 50's shows like "My Three

Sons" or "Father Knows Best." It relieved him to finally see the judge and hopefully clear up the confusion; at the very least, he was expecting to get out on bail.

"Good morning," said the judge.

The U.S. Attorneys corrected him that it was the afternoon and proceeded to give their formal introduction. "This is a matter involving the arrest of a material witness, Brandon Mayfield," the attorney began.

As he shifted in his seat and leaned slightly forward over the large wooden pulpit, the judge asked, "Has he been provided information as to the search warrant?"

"He has not been provided with the affidavit for the search warrant, your honor," the man responded.

"The returns on the search warrants, I assume, have not come in?"

"They have not, your honor. I would assume it would probably be Monday before the agents would be prepared to provide the court a return on the search warrants."

The judge then turned his gaze to Mr. Mayfield. "All right. First of all, if you would please, state your full name for the record."

"Your honor, my name is Brandon Mayfield," he said.

Then Judge Jones, before doing anything else, delivered a document to him regarding the recently-decided Awadallah case. He explained that the case was relevant to material witness proceedings and instructed him to read through it. The opinion, which Brandon would later read in more detail, laid out the purpose of the material witness statute. While the material witness statute was intended to secure testimony from individuals suspected of possible flight, it has been used in recent years to detain criminal suspects. The particular problem is that a material witness is expected to speak in court, even at the risk of perjury, and may be held in contempt of court for opting to remain silent. While Brandon, in theory, had the right to remain silent, exercising that right in a grand jury trial might result in his being held in contempt. Speaking up, and especially denying the validity of the fingerprint match, could be used against Brandon as being a false statement. While he knew the fingerprint was not his, the forensic science was stacked against him. Whether he spoke to deny it (and risked perjury) or remained silent (and risked contempt), Brandon faced imprisonment. It was the perfect catch-22.[9]

Judge Jones reminded him, "You have a right to remain silent, and as I understand it you have already invoked your right to remain silent to the government officers that arrested you. Essentially, we are looking at you as a person who is a practicing attorney in the state. You've served your government in two capacities, both as an enlisted man and an officer, and your fingerprint has been found on an article in Spain containing detonators."

Already, Brandon was perturbed by the implication of guilt and would not stand for such a bias. Brandon interrupted the judge. "That's not my fingerprint, your honor."

Taken by surprise, the judge momentarily fumbled. "I am just trying to relate what essentially has been said is your connection with...is your fingerprint on...is it a knapsack?"

"Blue plastic bag, your honor," the U.S. attorney interjected.

The Judge went on. "What were you going to say? It wasn't your fingerprint?"

Brandon replied. "If it was, I don't know how it got there." He then paused for a second, reflected on all possibilities, and said as clearly, distinctly, and unequivocally as he could the fact he knew to be true but that no one else could seem to accept. "It is not my fingerprint."

At that, the judge warned him that anything he said could be used against him, even to the extent that any response he gave might consist of an inconsistent or false statement. Brandon asked the Judge to give Tom and him a moment to confer, and Judge Jones graciously allowed them to use his chambers. While Tom and Brandon were just starting to talk, however, Tom got a call on his cellphone.

"I'd better get this," he said. "Hello...Yeah, this is he...From where? No...No, I can't answer that...No. Bye."

"Who was that?" Brandon inquired.

"Mike Isikoff from Newsweek magazine, asking if I have heard anything about your arrest." They both looked at each other in amazement, shocked that the media knew Tom was representing him. They had told no one.

They reconvened in the courtroom shortly thereafter and Brandon immediately turned his attention to the more pressing details of his detainment.

He addressed the judge. "I understand I have an opportunity to give perpetuation testimony today, and there is a possibility that I could remain here detained and give testimony in front of a grand jury. It may be that we can't get the grand jury to meet until as late as June 1st, correct?"

Judge Jones responded in the affirmative but insisted that he would try and get a grand jury in before June. That could mean more than three weeks rotting away in jail. What about his work? His family? What about bail? Surely, there would be bail. Jail was no pleasant place, but he especially could not go long without seeing his three kids and wife. They all meant the world to him, and without them his life would shatter. As he panicked at the prospect of three weeks just to get a jury, he hoped for a quick release on bond.

The words that then came from the judge's mouth were anathema to Brandon. "In the meantime I would be compelled, based upon the evidence that has been presented by affidavit—when you have your fingerprint on a key item of evidence and it has been verified by at least three experts as your fingerprint—to hold you here in custody for that period of time." No bail! He hadn't even made his case yet.

Brandon felt the dark walls of injustice and incarceration closing in around him, but he could not accept being locked up without having done anything wrong. He remembered the affidavit the agents had presented the Judge and pled, in an effort to change his mind. "Is it possible I could be released if I wear an ankle bracelet or something to that effect? I have a problem with this affidavit. I looked at it. I assume you have looked at it. We are talking about a fingerprint that was provided by the Spanish Police. That was a photograph of a latent print on this alleged bag. I have never seen this bag. I have no awareness about the bag that they are talking about," he continued, swallowing the nervousness that was choking up his throat. "There is a photograph. We don't have a chain of evidence. It is not the federal police that conducted the investigation gathering this alleged fingerprint and this alleged bag. It was provided to somebody here. I read the affidavit. There was some conflict about their matching fingerprint." Didn't the judge realize there was some doubt as to the veracity of the identification? And the rest of the evidence was circumstantial at best, irrelevant and religiously biased at worst?

At this, the Judge coldly said, "Your detention will not be based upon guilt or innocence. It will be based upon your testimony. It won't be based upon the government's case except to the extent, on a prima facie matter, they have established this fingerprint." He went on to explain a disturbing fact. "Now, I recognize fingerprints can be challenged and have been. In fact, a major case we had was with Steve Houze thirty years ago in 1974, a quadruple murder case, and a lot was involved with one fingerprint in the Colins Hawkins case. That man is still serving life imprisonment because of one fingerprint that was verified. So it is strong circumstantial evidence until it is rebutted." Life in prison for one fingerprint? What about mistakes? And if a man was found guilty of murder based on a fingerprint alone that means he could have been facing a death penalty. Brandon's heart raced.

Finding himself unable to accept he was being incarcerated and having failed to make a rational bid for his release, Brandon made a second, more human plea. "Your honor, I am a sole-practitioner here in Portland. I meet clients daily. I do domestic relations suits. I have clients I need to assist and file dissolutions. It was embarrassing being arrested." He went on. "This is circumstantial evidence. I guess what I was pleading for doesn't look like it is going to happen. I was hoping you could re-serve me—they could have served me a subpoena and I would have showed up on June 1st. I don't think it is necessary to detain me. I am an officer of the Court. I have a case before Judge Brown, an ERISA complaint here in District Court." He was losing his patience and repeated. "I am an officer of this Court. To me, this is embarrassing. It is humiliating. I am amazed I am arrested and before you in this court. And as I was arrested..." He then looked and pointed to the shadows in the back of the courtroom. "I don't know everybody back there. I know the officers who arrested me at my office. As I was arrested, I asked that they take the cuffs off me. They graciously put them in front of me." He looked between the Judge and the agents standing in the back. "When we were in the Ford Explorer, I said I didn't want to make a big scene. His reaction was that the media is close behind. Why was the media close behind? This can ruin my reputation. If Newsweek is going to be here and I'm detained, I have zero credibility with my clients."

The Judge's reply was flat and unapologetic. "We anticipate that this will have a substantial amount of publicity and that your name will be prominent. That will not be the product of either the prosecution or the Court. But I have to look at the whole picture. We are looking at a very serious situation. I will have to hold you." There was no way out. Brandon Mayfield was being physically constrained against his will, treated like a common criminal—no, a very uncommon criminal, and there was absolutely nothing he could do about it.

As Brandon was being led out of the courtroom by the marshals, he glanced over to the U.S. attorneys' table at the beaming looks of satisfaction, pride, and triumph on the faces of the people who had just secured his incarceration. Clutching closely to the legal opinion the Judge just handed him, he told Tom with a tone of urgency, "Call the Federal Public Defender's Office and get me the best attorney they have." The train to a death penalty had just pulled out of the station.

§ § §

Under Attorney General John Ashcroft's tenure there were a string of failed terrorist prosecutions across the country, from Tampa to Lackawanna, Detroit to Chicago, and from Boise to Portland. On September 2, 2004 a Federal Judge in Michigan threw out the only jury conviction the Justice Department had obtained under Ashcroft.[10] It was against three North African men from Detroit. Ashcroft held a national press conference touting the October, 2001, arrests of these three men as evidence of the success of his anti-terror campaign. But upon their release, there was no apologizing to the defendants who spent nearly three years in jail.

The government had originally charged the men with planning terrorist attacks but could never specify what activity they were involved in. One of the key witnesses turned out to have received a generous plea deal, and other key witnesses admitted to lying.[11]

Until its reversal, the Detroit case was the only terrorist conviction from the Justice Department's more than 5,000 foreigners detained in "anti-terrorism" sweeps since 9/11.[12] Ashcroft amazingly left his post as Attorney General with an astounding record of 0 for 5,000.[13] After 9/11, he frequently boasted about how many "suspected terrorists" had been detained, but never mentioned that exactly none turned out to be terrorists after all.[14] None of them were ever charged with a terror-related crime.

The government has also misused the material witness statute as a means to secure the indefinite incarceration of those it has wanted to investigate as possible terrorism suspects but for whom there was no real evidence against. Since September 11, 2001, at least seventy men living in the U.S.,[15] including Mayfield, all but one a Muslim, have found themselves in the Kafkaesque world of indefinite detention with no charges, secret evidence, and baseless accusations of terrorist links.[16]

The material witness statute adopted in 1984 was enacted to enable the government to secure the testimony of people who would otherwise flee the country to avoid testifying in court. But it has been misused by the Attorney General's office increasingly since 2001. In fact, on September 28, 2006, Federal District court judge Edward Lodge saw through the smoke and mirrors and ruled that the government could not use the material witness statute to detain people as suspects. Specifically, Judge Lodge stated: "The purpose of the material witness statute is to secure a material witness when it would be impractical to secure that witness through a subpoena...It would be improper for the government to use the material witness statute for other ends, such as the detention of persons suspected of criminal activity for which probable cause has not yet been established."[17]

The cost of these terrorism investigations is significant. Take for example the case of Sami Al-Arian, the former computer science professor at the University of Florida. When he was first indicted, John Ashcroft described Al-Arian and his organization as "responsible for the murders of dozens and dozens and dozens and dozens of people."[18] Apparently just using "dozens and dozens" was not dramatic enough. In December of 2005, after a long and costly jury trial, Al-Arian was acquitted of all of the serious charges and the jury hung on some of the lesser charges.

Sami Al-Arian's case cost Florida taxpayers an astounding (approximately) 30 million dollars.[19] A former Federal Prosecutor had this to say about the years of investigation and the outcome of the trial. "Very expensive proposition for the government and very little return for their dollar...9/11 we got scared. This indictment is the result of 9/11 and is another victim of 9/11." [20]

Since 9/11, approximately 195 suspected terrorists have been criminally convicted as of 2008 by a verdict or guilty plea,[21] while more than 500 suspects have been prosecuted for terrorism-related crimes in Federal courts.[22] However, several suspects were not involved in any terror-related plotting or financing at the time the government began investigating.[23] Moreover, the numbers can account for terrorism committed by groups other than al-Qaeda, such as Columbian Revolutionary armed forces and Tamil Tigers. Finally, a large number of prosecutions include individuals originally charged as terrorists under initial immigration sweeps but later charged with immigration or fraud charges.

Many of these prosecutions are attributable to well organized sting operations by undercover agents. For example, a report by the New York University School of Law Center for Human Rights and Global Justice (CHRGJ) describes how American counterterrorism efforts have singled out Muslim Americans by sending paid, trained informants into mosques and Muslim communities. The report found over 200 terrorism-related prosecutions have relied upon informants.[24]

The Center for Global Justice, along with many former FBI agents, lawmakers, and advocacy organizations, are all concerned that the police are creating their own "homegrown" terrorism plots, "foiling" them for the cameras, and sending Muslim Americans to prison; meanwhile, Americans are no safer from real terrorist threats and risk assaults to their freedom to practice religion and express ideas freely.[25]

An example of an unwitting participant in a government-created terrorist plot is Mohammed Osman, otherwise known as the Pioneer Courthouse Square Christmas tree bomber. Osman, a troubled Somali-American high school student, was contacted by the FBI after a tip-off, and over the span of nearly two years became involved in a plot to bomb spectators at a Christmas tree lighting in downtown Portland.[26] He was ultimately provided a fake bomb and arrested at the scene of his failed detonation attempt in November of 2010. According to the government's own affidavit, when asked by undercover agents for the first time what this recent high school graduate was going to do with his life, the young Somali American was silent.[27] Getting no response, the agent suggested various things, including going operational or becoming a martyr. There is no evidence that before that June 10, 2010, meeting with the undercover agent that Mohammed ever wanted to go operational or had any intention to harm anyone. To the contrary, the affidavit provides that during his second meeting with an agent, Mohammed revealed he had thought of committing violence, prayed for guidance on whether to act on it, had a dream, and decided against it.[28]

These sorts of cases are particularly troubling to the Muslim communities, many of which express concern that they are under heightened scrutiny and at risk of being targeted for sting operations. Sending informants, especially to mosques, creates an atmosphere of distrust and further feeds the ostracism that Muslims (particularly immigrants) feel as they assimilate into this country. While Mohamed Osman ultimately made a bad, dangerous decision that even the most troubled immigrant would likely not make (to detonate a presumed bomb at a busy gathering), one wonders if he could or would have ever come to the same decision without the instigation of the government.

§ § §

[1] *In re Federal Grand Jury 03-01*, No. 04-MC-9071 (D. Or. Filed May 6, 2004) (Richard Werder Affidavit for material witness arrest warrant).

[2] "Ashland-based Islamic charity Al-Haramain pleads guilty to tax fraud, charges dropped against Pete Seda." OregonLive. 29 July 2014. Web. 31 Aug. 2014. <http://www.oregonlive.com/pacific-northwest-news/index.ssf/2014/07/ashland-based_islamic_charity.html>.

[3] Uniting and Strengthening America by Providing Appropriate Tools Required to Intercept and Obstruct Terrorism Act of 2001, Pub. L. No. 107-56, 115 Stat. 272, § 215 (2001) (enacted Oct. 26, 2001).

[4] "The President on Mass Surveillance." The New York Times. 17 Jan. 2014. Web. 1 Sept. 2014. <http://www.nytimes.com/2014/01/18/opinion/the-president-on-mass-surveillance.html>.

[5] Horwitz, Sari, and William Branigin. "Lawmakers of both parties voice doubts about NSA surveillance programs." The Washington Post. 17 July 2013. Web. 1 Sept. 2014. <http://www.washingtonpost.com/world/national-security/house-committee-holds-hearing-on-nsa-surveillance-programs/2013/07/17/ffc3056c-eee3-11e2-9008-61e94a7ea20d_story.html>.

[6] *Id.*

[7] Note that key provisions of the Patriot Act, including Section 215, were set to expire June 1, 2015. Shortly thereafter, Congress passed the USA Freedom Act, which was touted as essentially ending bulk phone records collection. Contemporaneously, the FISC ruled that it was lawful for the government to continue bulk collection for a 5-month transition period, despite Congress' clear intent to end such collection.

[8] Wyden, Ron, Mark Udall, and Martin Heinrich. "End the N.S.A. Dragnet, Now."The New York Times. 25 Nov. 2013. Web. 1 Sept. 2014. <http://www.nytimes.com/2013/11/26/opinion/end-the-nsa-dragnet-now.html>.

[9] See the chapter entitled "The Awadallah Predicament" for a more complete discussion of the material witness statute.

[10] Jeralyn. "Ashcroft: Not a Single Post 9/11 Terror Conviction - TalkLeft: The Politics Of Crime." TalkLeft. 22 Sept. 2004. Web. 30 Aug. 2014. <http://www.talkleft.com/story/2004/09/22/699/02879/waronterror/Ashcroft-Not-a-Single-Post-9-11-Terror-Conviction>. (Quoting Georgetown Law Professor David Cole).

[11] Slevin, Peter. "Detroit 'Sleeper Cell' Prosecutor Faces Probe." The Washington Post. The Washington Post, 20 Nov. 2005. Web. 29 Aug. 2014. <http://www.washingtonpost.com/wp-dyn/content/article/2005/11/19/AR2005111900952_2.html>.

[12] Jeralyn. "Ashcroft: Not a Single Post 9/11 Terror Conviction - TalkLeft: The Politics Of Crime." TalkLeft. 22 Sept. 2004. Web. 30 Aug. 2014. <http://www.talkleft.com/story/2004/09/22/699/02879/waronterror/Ashcroft-Not-a-Single-Post-9-11-Terror-Conviction>. (Quoting Georgetown Law Professor David Cole).

[13] *Id.*

[14] *Id.*

[15] See Human Rights Watch June 2005 Vol. 17, No. 2 (G). Witness to Abuse Human Rights Abuses under the Material Witness Law since September 11.

[16] For example, 34-year-old graduate student from Boise Idaho, Sami Al Hussayn, was charged with aiding a terrorist group for volunteer work he did, maintaining a website for a North American Islamic

organization. His case was tried by a jury and he was acquitted in June of 2004. One of the witnesses in that case, Abdullah Al-kid was on his way to study in Saudi Arabia when he was arrested March 16, 2003 at Dulles international airport as a material witness where he was shackled, chained, and held for 16 days before being released to over a year of probation and travel restrictions. See O'Hagan, Maureen. "A terrorism case that went awry." The Seattle Times. 22 Nov. 2004. Web. 30 Aug. 2014. <http://seattletimes.com/html/localnews/2002097570 _sami22m.html> and Serrano, Richard. "Detained for years but never charged." Las Vegas Sun, 5 Nov. 2009. Web. 30 Aug. 2014. <http:// www.lasvegassun.com/news/2009/nov/05/who-responsible-his-nightmare/>.

[17] Order of United States District Court for the District of Idaho-Kidd v. Gonzales-Case 1:05-cv-00093-EJL-MHW Document 351 Filed 09/27/12. Page 5 of 13.

[18] Deeson, Mike. "Al-Arian case costs millions." *10News*. 7 Dec. 2005. Web. 30 Aug. 2014. <http://archive.wtsp.com/news/story.aspx? storyid=22327>.

[19] *Id.*

[20] *Id.*

[21] Zabel, Richard, and James Benjamin. "In Pursuit of Justice." *Humanrightsfirst.org*. Human Rights First, 1 July 2009. Web. 14 Mar. 2015. <http://www.humanrightsfirst.org/wp-content/uploads/ pdf/090723-LS-in-pursuit-justice-09-update.pdf>.

[22] Human Rights Watch. "Illusion of Justice." Jul. 2014. Web. 14. Mar. 2015. Page 2. <http://www.hrw.org/sites/default/files/reports/ usterrorism0714_ForUpload_0_0_0.pdf>

[23] *Id.*

[24] Center for Human Rights and Global Justice, Targeted and Entrapped: Manufacturing the "Homegrown Threat" in the United States (New York: NYU School of Law, 2011). 2.

[25] *Id.* at 4.

[26] See McCall, William, and Nedra Pickler. "Feds: Sting snares man planning to bomb tree-lighting ceremony." KATU. 27 Nov. 2010. Web. 30 Aug. 2014. <http://www.katu.com/news/local/ 110898914.html>

[27] See affidavit here: http://media.katu.com/
documents/1+Affidavit+COMPLAINT+11+26.pdf
[28] *Id.*

Chapter 8
Containing the Situation

"O you who have believed, do not enter houses other than your own houses until you ascertain welcome and greet their inhabitants. That is best for you; perhaps you will be reminded." Koran 24:27.

Mona had just hung up the phone with Brandon when she noticed between the cracks in the living room blinds two figures dressed in dark business attire approaching the entrance. Like Brandon, she assumed the two were solicitors and went to grab a headscarf before hearing a loud knock. She tucked her curly, thick hair under the scarf, quickly put on her glasses and made herself just barely presentable. As a low-maintenance woman she would never think to wear makeup, and being blessed with even-toned tan skin she did not need to. Dressed comfortably in pajamas and expecting the ensuing encounter to be short, she creaked open the door and poked her head out.

"Hi." She addressed the man and woman with a hint of "who are you and what do you want" in her voice.

Immediately, the two flashed their FBI badges and said they were there to ask her some questions.

"No thanks," Mona declined. "I'm not even fully dressed," and she slowly began to close the door.

"Open the door! Open the door—we have a warrant!" the FBI agents yelled at her.

Reluctantly, she stood in the doorway, irked by the fact that she wasn't dressed appropriately and was obliged to cooperate with these strangers.

"Have you heard about what happened in Madrid, Spain, the horrible act that happened? Your husband's fingerprint was found on a bag near the detonation site and he has been identified as a material witness."

Mona immediately refuted their claim. "It's a mistake. It's impossible. Give me a moment," she said, slamming the door shut. What the hell were they talking about? Mona thought back to the day the terrorist attack had occurred in Madrid, Spain. She vaguely remembered the family gathering for dinner. Brandon was at home that night, carrying a plate of food into the living room to watch the breaking news with her. The initial reports stated that powerful explosions had torn through three Madrid trains during the morning rush hour with reports of up to 173 dead, and that the attack was likely committed by a Basque separatist group known as the ETA. Then, almost inexplicably, it was reported that the Spanish police had found an abandoned white van in Alcala de Henares, near the station where the bombed trains had passed through. Inside it were seven detonators and a cassette tape with verses of the Koran. Brandon and Mona were both grieved by the loss of innocent lives and infuriated that a fellow Muslim may have committed the crime. Mona remembered Brandon telling her that he did not care if it was Basque or Muslims who did it and they were "criminals of the lowest order to attack innocent people on commuter trains." There was simply no justification.

It was impossible, Mona thought, that he could have been even remotely connected to the attacks, let alone a material witness. She concluded that whatever the FBI had surmised must have been in total error.

Frenzied and confused, Mona reached for her cellphone and tried to call Brandon. No answer. The FBI agents, aware that she was attempting to call him, started shouting. "Look, we can break down the door! We have a search warrant." Mona did not move a muscle, still shocked. After a short pause, they added, "Your husband is being arrested right now!" Mona froze and felt a choking in her heart. Arrested? She had no choice but to let them in.

They ordered her to walk them through the house to see if anyone else was there. The agents asked her where she wanted to sit during the search, cautioning that she could not move from that spot during its entire duration. One of the FBI agents explained to her that it was called "containing the situation." She decided to sit at the kitchen table, which was situated centrally between the living room, the bathroom and her bedroom. Not able to anticipate how long the search would last, Mona asked to use the restroom. She, an independent and autonomous woman, felt ridiculous having to ask permission for such menial thing.

"Yes, but we will have to conduct a search of it first," an agent responded.

Mona was quick in the restroom, fearful that one of the agents would come in had she taken too long. When she came out, the FBI agents started asking questions, probing her for details about Brandon. Mona insisted that she wasn't interested. Visibly irritated, the male agent taunted her. "What do you have to hide? Huh?"

"My husband is innocent!" she yelled. "If you insist on asking questions I want my lawyer."

An agent then asked her with feigned innocence, "You have a lawyer? Why would you need a lawyer? Why would you need one? Why don't you just talk to us?" Mona, distrusting of him, said she had nothing to hide but invoked her right to an attorney.

The resilient male agent then opened up his briefcase and pulled out a small blue bag. "Have you seen this bag before? This bag was at the scene. This is the bag your husband's fingerprints were found on. Have you seen this bag or a bag like this?"

"I don't recognize it. Is that the actual bag?" Surely it couldn't be.

"No, but one just like it was found at the scene. Are you sure you haven't seen this bag?" The interrogation continued until the ringing home phone interrupted. Mona's immediate response was to jump up but she restrained herself.

"Can I get that?"

"No, we cannot allow that," the female agent chimed in. After an excruciating ten seconds or so, the answering machine sounded with a familiar voice. It was Brandon's mother, back in Kansas.

"Hello, it's Avnell. The FBI was just at my house asking questions. Please call me back." Mona knew that she was not the only one being interrogated and that multiple family members were probably being involved. That only meant one thing: it was a big deal, whatever it was.

The agents must have seen Avnell as no threat because when the phone rang again soon after, they assumed it was her and allowed Mona to answer. This time, however, it was Michael Isikoff from Newsweek, calling at the most inopportune time and disappointing Mona who wished it was Avnell.

"Hello, this is Michael Isikoff from Newsweek. We heard Brandon Mayfield has been arrested. Would you like to comment?"

She thought of answering, "Sorry, my house is being raided by the FBI right now. No can do." Incredulous of him knowing about the whole occasion and acutely aware that she probably should not make any public statements so prematurely, Mona instead responded that she could not talk and abruptly ended the call.

"That was Michael Isikoff from Newsweek. How did they know about the arrest here?" The female agent shrugged her shoulders and the male agent ignored her completely.

After the two agents finished questioning her temporarily and just as Mona's patience was wearing thin, ten to twelve more agents entered the house. It was as if a SWAT team was busting in, ready to disengage some hidden bomb. Perhaps it was in the bathroom, or in the kitchen, or under the bed, or in the bag drawer, or in the garbage can, or in the recycling bin, or in the flour! The agents searched everything in the house meticulously and methodically, but with reckless execution. Items such as clothes were thrown to the ground from their drawers, papers were scattered without order, and the pantry was left as though a starving army had passed through it. Nothing was spared inspection. One after the other, inspectors spilled into each room, rechecking the same areas over and over.

Meanwhile, Mona was still stuck at the kitchen table with the original two agents. As they were nearly finished with their interrogation, one of them stated rather frankly, "We've been following you." The words resonated, seeming to Mona as though they belonged in a cheesy, low-budget film. A low-budget horror film, that is. But they raised a real question: how long had the FBI been following the family? And who exactly had the agents been following?

"Have you been following my kids?" she finally brought herself to ask.

"No, not your children."

Good.

§ § §

The hours passed slowly, punctuated by occasional questions and remarks from the two agents: 11 am, 12 pm, 1 pm, and 2 pm. Before long, Mona realized that she would have to leave to pick up the children from school as the FBI were still not done with the search.

The agents insisted that they go to the schools with her, but she vehemently rejected their "gracious offer." Bringing them would terrify the children, who still had no knowledge of the ordeal. Mona was already traumatized by the FBI's forceful intrusion and did not want them to be there when she had to break the news to the kids.

"Look, I need my keys to get the kids." Begrudgingly, an FBI agent slid off two keys from Mona's keychain: one for the van and one for the house.

"Okay, but we're going to have to check your purse and your van." After searching her vehicle, purse, checkbook and wallet, and even confiscating photos of her nephew, they allowed her to go. But they warned Mona that once she left the premise, she could not re-enter the house until the search was complete, implying that she might have to find another place to stay.

As Mona pulled out of the driveway, she felt both relieved and dizzied. Mostly, she was glad to be out of the house and escape the unrelenting interrogation. But there was an eerie premonition in the back of her head that, despite Brandon's innocence, the odds would not be in his favor. On the way to school, Mona dialed the only person she could think of for help, both legal and emotional: Tom Nelson.

When Tom's assistant picked up, Mona swallowed her tears and asked that he relay a brief message: "Tell Tom, there's...there's a horrible emergency and ask that he call me back ASAP." Just as she pressed the red end-call button on her cell phone, Mona burst out crying, unable to contain herself. The graveness of the situation was sinking in; despite her background working in a law office, she needed legal counsel. She knew Brandon needed counsel too. The drive to Sunset High School was longer than the average 20 minutes; it seems like an eternity as she mulled over all the possibilities. Perhaps Brandon was framed. Perhaps he somehow touched a blue bag that made its way to Spain. Perhaps the forensic scientist made a mistake.

§ § §

Mona had three children to pick up, one each in elementary, middle, and high school. Shane, fifteen, was the first in the queue and the oldest. He was the cool and confident kid and had only recently gotten his "man" voice after one year of an embarrassing high-pitched transition from his boy one. He shaved off his "Arab-fro" (as he called it) and now had short crispy black hair. He rarely smiled, his pursed lips of resolve smothered in Vaseline because, in his words, "ChapStick was for girls." Both he and his younger brother Samir were tan and looked more Egyptian like their mother Mona, although Shane's slender nose and square jaw were clearly Brandon's. As for Samir, ten, he was an aspiring singer and entertainer with few inhibitions, the so-called "clown" of the family. He had a full head of bouncy curls and was underweight for his age, his ribs and sternum poking through the taut skin wrapped around his midsection. Because he was slightly taller than his peers, his clothing never fit quite right. He wore jeans one size smaller than for his age and even then had to use a belt to hold them up, his ankles awkwardly sticking out from the bottom of the pant legs. Sharia, the middle child, age 12, was unlike her brothers, a proud but timid nerd. She was fair-skinned like her father with medium brown hair that she tucked neatly under a headscarf when in public. She had volitionally donned the hijab, following the 9/11 attacks, to let others know she was not ashamed of being Muslim.

§ § §

Shane was waiting in the high school parking lot as Mona pulled in 10 minutes later than usual. Immediately he suspected that something was wrong, as Mona was usually very timely. As he approached the vehicle, he noticed she was visibly upset, wiping away tears with the sleeve of her shirt.

"Mom, what's wrong?" he asked.

She sniffled and blurted, "Your dad was arrested!"

"Arrested? No way!" Shane laughed in disbelief.

Mona held out an FBI card one of the agents had handed her during the search and iterated, "They arrested your dad."

Shane grabbed the card, still unaware of the details, and began to cry.

§ § §

Sharia was in the Meadow Park middle school library for class when she was called to the front office. Excited to leave early, she anxiously grabbed her backpack and rushed out. Mona had gone in to sign her out, but by the time Sharia got there she was back in the van bawling. Instead, Shane was sent in to break the news to her. He wore a sullen, stern expression that worried Sharia, whose mind was already plagued with fear. Why was he here? Before she could ask any questions, Shane whispered, "Let's go. Something happened to dad." Sharia trailed a foot behind him as he hurried out of the school's doors.

"What happened? What happened to dad! Tell me what happened." She demanded answers but was faced with cruel silence. Finally, Shane—bothered by her incessant demands—stopped walking and turned to her. "Dad was arrested by the FBI." A weight lifted off Sharia's heart. She had thought he had gotten in an accident or, worse, had died.

Then, as was the case with Shane, a wave of disbelief set in. "Arrested by the FBI? What is this, an action movie?" He ignored her, but it was clear when she got to the van that something was wrong. Mona was crying and talking to Brandon's brother Kent on the cellphone as Sharia slid open the van door. Shane climbed into the passenger's seat and fought back tears. Sharia, overwhelmed by the emotion in the van, and in want of answers, also joined in mourning. Surely, if her mom was broken down in tears, something very terrible must have happened, she reasoned. Mona rarely ever cried in front of the children, always wanting to be a beacon of strength and composure for them. But in that moment of complete despair, Mona could think of nothing but the prospect of Brandon—innocent and undeserving of such a fate—in jail.

§ § §

Samir was the only one left and Mona was late in picking him up. He was waiting patiently near the principal's office, and Shane was again designated to go inside. A similar scenario unraveled as Samir's first response to the shocking news was incredulousness. "No, you're joking, Shane." But it was no joke.

As he too entered the caravan of despair, he angrily shouted, "You're not lying, you're not lying, you're not lying!" and burst out sobbing.

Mona was very frank with the children and explained, "I don't know why this is happening or what is going on." As the children fought for more details, Mona finally divulged the little bit that she knew. "He was arrested for those train bombings. You remember back in March? There was a train bombing in Madrid, Spain. He's arrested as a material witness."

A sense of relief overcame the van. They did not know what a material witness meant and they did not care. "Oh, so it's just a big mistake. He should be out soon then," Sharia stated, incognizant of the "100%" fingerprint match and 100% certain that her dad had nothing to do with the bombing.

Mona was more mature, though, and knew that legal proceedings took time even when the defendant was completely innocent. She thought to herself that everything would be cleared up by the start of the following week. The judge might be busy but surely four days was enough to rectify the mistake. Yet, even the thought of Brandon in jail for four full days made her shiver. And what if it took even longer? She could not entertain such a thought.

It was a surreal moment as the family reached home again. Mona expected the FBI to be gone by the time she returned and was right. It was quiet. The sun was shining, the air was crisp and the house, at least from the outside, was just like usual. The white side panels were bright and clean. The grass was trimmed short. The van was parked where it was before. Everything seemed normal. But inside, inside the house, things were falling apart at the seams. The FBI had made no effort to maintain any semblance of order. Papers were scattered, food packages opened; every inch of the house was probed, exposed, and examined. Computer hard-drives were copied, search histories collected, and personal correspondences read. Yellow post-its labeled each room alphabetically, furniture was rearranged, and the cats were locked in closets or bedrooms without access to food or water. Everything was in complete disarray, and the mark of an unwelcomed guest was impossible to ignore.

Samir and Shane brought themselves to their feet and slowly walked toward the entrance as though some agent was about to jump out of a rose bush. Sharia stepped onto the green grass and curled into a ball, her sobbing eyes forming wet blobs on the knees of her jeans. Mona, in awe of what had transpired, said in a voice barely audible to her sons, "I want to set this house on fire; that's what I want to do." And she wasn't alone. The children did not know what to expect inside, but there was an uneasy feeling that something was not the same—an unspoken understanding that the house was an extension of the family and that the search did not just expose the secrets of the house itself but violated each family member in a personal and humiliating way. From that moment on, the house was just a house. Mona and the kids would never see it as a home again.

Chapter 9
All Jacked Up

"No snowflake in an avalanche ever feels responsible." Voltaire

After leaving the courtroom, Brandon was quickly ushered down to the basement of the Federal Courthouse for processing. Underground, there was a maze of chain-link doors as well as small rooms and a marshal awaiting his arrival. Almost immediately the marshal, a young, dark-haired man of medium stature, asked for Brandon's name and address.

"Brandon Mayfield..." he began.

"Oh, I'm Brandon too," the marshal interrupted. Marshal Brandon, of amiable disposition, revealed that he had served in the Marines.

"Well, that makes two Brandon vets. I served in the army," Mr. Mayfield told him, and they exchanged an unspoken recognition of each other's commitment to our country. Two soldiers. Two Brandons. Two different worlds. It was a strange moment: here they were chatting as if nothing else mattered. But in a few minutes he would be gone and shuffling through paperwork, preparing for the next inmate. Did he think Mr. Mayfield was a criminal? Was he chatting out of pity, affording Mr. Mayfield some last vestige of normalcy? After a few minutes, the marshal pushed forward on the counter an electronic contraption resembling an oversized calculator.

As he was preparing the machine, Marshal Brandon told Brandon Mayfield he would be transferred to the Multnomah County Detention Center.

"You're going to take me outside?" Mr. Mayfield asked.

"Yeah. It's not very far to the detention center."

Brandon thought about the call from Newsweek to Tom in the courtroom and surmised there was probably press waiting to pounce. "I don't feel safe going to the detention center."

"What do you mean?" the marshal asked.

"I mean I'm concerned that someone might take a pot shot at me because you guys created a situation that could put my physical safety in jeopardy."

The marshal left shortly then came back. "Has anyone called you Brian or Randy? You know, because it sounds kind of like Brandon. It happens to me sometimes."

"On occasion," Mr. Mayfield admitted. "I have been mistakenly called Brian. Why?"

"We're going to give you the pseudonym Randy Taylor. None of the inmates will know who you are. We'll let the detention center front desk know."

"Randy Taylor," Mr. Mayfield repeated to himself. It sounded so generic and unoriginal, but he knew he had better embrace it and grow responsive to it if that was to be his new identity.

The marshal motioned him over to the copy machine contraption. "I need to take your prints."

"Do I have to or is it an option?" Mr. Mayfield asked.

"Well, it's standard procedure," he replied.

"You can probably get a court order to require me to do it anyway. Besides I am sure you have my original print cards somewhere." Brandon rolled his hands, fingers, and thumb on a screen that recorded the image; there was no ink. When Marshal Brandon asked him to sign a piece of paper acknowledging the prints he resisted. "Can anyone subpoena these prints?"

"No, nobody can use these. The FBI can't have them, we don't share them with anybody, and they're just for our purposes." Not fully convinced and afraid he had already been framed, he agreed to sign them if it was dated by him and included the marshal's signature as well. As Marshal Brandon signed the print card and finalized the paperwork, Brandon Mayfield thought about another Brandon, himself twenty years ago, and how a bizarre series of events one cold winter's night helped give the government the justification they needed to turn his world upside down.

§ § §

Brandon grew up in rural Kansas. His mom and dad divorced when he was eleven, and since that time he lived with his mom and two brothers, Mike and Kent, in a dilapidated, old, two-story farm house pretty much in the middle of nowhere. Upon turning seventeen, Brandon decided to live with his father in Halstead, the self-proclaimed "biggest little city in Kansas." As small rural communities go, Halstead, population 2,000, was more progressive than most and boasted not just one but two beer joints. In the fall of 1984, Brandon, having graduated high school, enrolled in classes at Hutchinson Community College with little interest in his subjects. He began drinking frequently on weekends to the point of occasional belligerence. During winter break, on a particularly cold night, he and some of the locals decided to head into Wichita looking for "something to do."

The driver of the old Chevy four-door had a bottle of whiskey under his seat that he kindly shared with Brandon and the two girls and a guy in the back seat. The car, with the windows half fogged, reeked of booze and cigarettes. After a bite to eat and cruising the streets they decided to head back, but not before they set their eyes upon a small convertible parked along the curb in front of a small ranch style home. It was the perfect target: completely dark except for Christmas lights. They wanted to roll the car but Brandon was not up to it.

Brandon stared out of the Chevy as his friends managed, with some effort, to roll the small car on its side, run back to the Chevy, spin the wheels, and leave. It was sometime between night and morning as they started back to Halstead. The guy driving was quite liquored up by that time. He attempted to enter the freeway on-ramp much too fast, and the car skidded and launched airborne off the embankment, taking out a chain link fence in the process.

The car, with a blown tire from the impact, came to rest atop the crushed fence at the bottom of the embankment. Luckily no one was injured. Unluckily, the car had no jack to allow them to put on the spare tire. It felt like ten below outside, and none of them were dressed for the occasion. Fresh snow had piled up several inches high. Brandon told the girls to wait in the car while he and the two other guys searched for help. There were only a few houses several blocks away, but when they knocked no one answered. Brandon wandered off to an industrial building nearby and peered inside, but the doors were locked and the lights were off. In the parking lot in front of the building was a small Dodge Colt station wagon. Brandon saw through the rear window a car jack lying in plain view, as if sent from heaven. He did a three-sixty scan of the area: snow, gray night sky, no one around for miles but them, nothing in sight, and there in front of him a car jack. It seemed surreal. He did not hesitate. He busted the rear window and took the jack.

The guys had the car up on the jack in no time. They were just about to replace the spare and be off when a squad car pulled up with its sirens flashing. The officers asked what the hooligans were doing. The driver explained that he slid off the ramp because the road conditions were slippery. One of the officers shined his flashlight down at the jack and then back in the boys' faces and asked where the jack for the car came from. No one said a word. It was a tense moment. There was a long, uncomfortable silence, and then Brandon confessed. He could not lie. He had taken the jack because they were cold and stranded and were unable to find any help. It was his fault; he had, in a moment of haste and despair, stolen the jack. Immediately, the officers took him by the arm to the squad car where they frisked him, read him his rights, and transported him to Sedgewick County jail to be booked and fingerprinted.

At the station, Brandon was placed temporarily into a holding cell next to a drunken man asleep on the tiny bench against the wall. The place smelled of vomit, and there were the sounds of mumbling and snoring. After a phone call to his father in a plea to come get him, Brandon was then fingerprinted. He was escorted to a small table around the corner at the end of the hall lit by a single incandescent bulb. Some men brought out the ink pad and told him to relax as they rolled each finger individually over the pad and then again over the print card with its box for each digit. Brandon looked at the impressions and thought about finger painting as a child with his mother.

The car, as it turned out, belonged to the security guard working in the building outside the on-ramp. Brandon paid the guard and got a young public defender to work out a deal. In exchange for dropping the charges, Brandon promised he would join the Army, swearing to defend and protect the Constitution of the United States. He wanted adventure, but not in the bottom of whiskey bottles.

Chapter 10
Detention and Defense

"The man who asks a question is a fool for a minute, the man who does not ask is a fool for life." Confucius

The holding area of the Multnomah County Detention Center looked like a DMV waiting area, and Brandon anxiously scanned the room for a seat. As he sat down and waited, he heard someone call out, "Is Mr. Taylor here?"

Brandon hesitated before remembering his pseudonym, saying "yeah" at the same time with another Mr. Taylor. Everyone looked around and laughed. How comical that two men with the "same" name were about to be imprisoned, Brandon thought. A group of men were then called to stand behind a red line, in single file, until their name was called for a mug shot to be taken. The guard at the photo counter called the name Taylor (the other Taylor was in a separate line) and Brandon stood there unaccustomed to his pseudonym. A frail black man with sagging blood-shot eyes gave Brandon a gentle prod. "Go, dude, that's you. Don't you know your own name?" Brandon stepped forward.

"Turn to the left. Turn to the right."

After being photographed, the men gathered in a larger general processing area with phones and televisions mounted on the walls. It was like a greyhound bus station, except there were a few small, unoccupied holding cells. By the third time Brandon was called by name he responded to Taylor without hesitation. He went up to the administrator's desk where a man in black Buddy Holly glasses asked him, "Have you ever been in California, been in prison, and do you ever go by any name other than Rick Taylor?"

Brandon said a general no to all the questions but was suspicious it might have been a trap; his name was supposed to be Randy Taylor, and now he was being asked about Rick Taylor. Was he supposed to say, "Well, no, I'm Brandon Mayfield?" It was too late to correct himself and Brandon did not want to bring up what he thought was a harmless error. He sat back down but was called a second time by the same man at the counter, who was pissed.

"You are not supposed to lie to us!" He then held up a printed news article with an unmistakable photo of Brandon. "You're Brandon Mayfield. You're going to pay for this. You're going to wish you hadn't lied to me!"

Brandon did not know how to react to this threat. Nobody had said whether he should tell anyone at the county jail about the pseudonym. He stood there dumbfounded and fearful. What was he supposed to have said? Tell the jail officials his real name even when he was in their system as Randy Taylor? Damned if he did, damned if he didn't.

Because of his seeming deception, Brandon was removed from the general area for processing and placed in a separate cell as punishment. They gave him a sack lunch for dinner—an apple and a soggy sandwich—but Brandon did not want to eat. He was not allowed to use the phone to contact his family, watch TV, or interact with other people. After a short time he was told to go to the dressing room. A husky man took Brandon into a storage area with stacked linens and clothes.

"Okay, put these on," the man said, handing him a folded jail uniform: blue linen bottoms with an elastic waist band, a short sleeve blue shirt with one breast pocket, and a pink t-shirt and boxer shorts, complete with a pair of plastic slippers.

Brandon was embarrassed standing there and looked around unsuccessfully for any nook or separate place to disrobe. All he could do was turn away from the man and get undressed and redressed. He was asked to put his civilian clothes and personal belongings in a bag. Brandon obeyed.

"That's it," Brandon said.

"The ring too," the guard said.

"What ring?" Brandon asked, and the man pointed at the silver wedding ring on his finger. Brandon reluctantly wiggled it off and slid it into the bag, the last souvenir from his free life. He was then led back to the holding cell and remained there until his attorney arrived.

§ § §

Brandon first met his publically-appointed lawyer in a visitation room much like the one at the courthouse but with only one stool. He was ambivalent to the man waiting for him that night—a big gregarious guy with a shiny, black leather jacket. With a hint of an east coast accent, he introduced himself. "Hi. Chris Schatz. I am from the Federal Public Defender's office. Tom called me and asked if I would come see you."

Brandon looked Chris slowly up and down, unsure if he could trust him to close the deal. As a fellow lawyer, and considering the stakes, Brandon knew he would need the best possible counsel he could get and immediately inquired of Chris's background.

Chris assured Brandon that he had 10 years of experience and that he could handle the case. Skeptical, Brandon asked, "What was the last big case you had?" He went on about some cases that Brandon, as a fairly informed lawyer, had never heard of.

"I'm talking what have you done that's big—high profile?" Brandon repeated, unconvinced that Chris would be of much help.

With that, Chris turned defensive, and rightfully so. He must have been surprised by the ingrate before him and made it clear he was not there to validate himself. "You have to tell me right now whether or not you want the public defenders' office, or we'll just go on our way." Chris had nothing to prove and nothing to lose by walking away.

But Brandon was not done with his interrogation. "Who do you work for? What's his name?"

"The head of the public defender's office, Steve Wax," [1] Chris answered, unamused by Brandon's scrutiny but polite and cooperative nonetheless.

Knowing the seriousness of the situation, and feeling that Chris at least appreciated his concern, Brandon recommended that Chris bring in Steve Wax so that they might both work on the high-profile case together. Brandon knew he needed more than one man on the case but was aware that a beggar could not be a chooser—especially when the beggar happened to be an alleged terrorist. Chris said he would contact Steve about the prospect of working on the case together and then began asking Brandon some routine background questions.

Before answering anything, Brandon hinted that he heard Attorney General Ashcroft had issued a directive allowing attorney-client conversations to be monitored for terrorist investigations. He asked Chris if their conversation was being recorded. Chris said they were supposed to be confidential, but he could not promise anything. The lack of privacy in his home, his office, and now in the detention center bothered Brandon immensely and seemed unfair. The FBI could listen in on any conversation he had, without notice, and yet afforded Brandon absolutely no transparency. To claim a power equivalency between him and the FBI would be an utter lie—its ludicrous self-entitlement coupled with its own furtiveness gave the FBI a serious advantage in forging a case against Brandon. Brandon wanted to talk without the phone and glass between him and Chris and was careful to divulge as little as possible until he was allowed a private face-to-face visitation.

Chris asked standard financial questions to determine if Brandon qualified for assistance. "How much money do you make a year? Do you have more than $10,000 in stocks, bonds, or bank accounts?" Brandon answered no to the latter question, which was technically true. He told Chris about his assets and cars, and wanted to tell him that he had placed close to $10,000 dollars in a safety deposit box just weeks before he was arrested because he thought he was being burglarized. He decided not to bring it up until he could arrange a more private visit with his attorneys. Brandon signed the legal service contract that Chris slid him and was cautioned that he would have to wait until Chris talked to Steve before knowing if he would receive public representation. There was no way Brandon could pay for a top attorney out of pocket.

The money in the safety deposit box was all he had. He was a young attorney struggling to build his new solo practice, barely able to make ends meet. Most of his clients were cash-strapped family law referrals from the Oregon State Bar's Modest Means program who he agreed to represent at significantly reduced rate. Representing low-income clients made it difficult for him to keep up with the lease and overhead for his small office. He just purchased a house with little equity and in constant need of repairs. He could not afford a private attorney even if he wanted to. He needed the public defenders even if it was all he could get.

§ § §

[1] Steven T. Wax, one of the country's long serving federal public defenders and top national security lawyers, later went on to defend several Guantanamo detainees and helped secure the release of Adel Hassan Hamad. Hamad was an innocent Sudanese detainee who spent over four grueling years at Camp X-Ray, during which time his young daughter died for lack of medical care. (See Wax's award-winning book *Kafka Comes to America: Fighting for Justice in the War on Terror—A Public Defender's Inside Account* for the full story). Wax announced his retirement from the Federal Public Defender's Office in April of 2014, after over 30 years of serving countless clients. He has joined the Oregon Innocence Project as the legal director of the newly-formed non-profit.

Chapter 11
First Day of Hell

"The media's the most powerful entity on earth. They have the power to make the innocent guilty and to make the guilty innocent, and that's power. Because they control the minds of the masses." Malcolm X.

On May 6, while Brandon was spending his first day in the detention center, Mona and the kids were in another kind of prison. Shortly after the family came home to a ransacked house Mona got a call from a family friend, and she knew the word was spreading fast. There had been no media contacting Mona up to that point except for the Michael Isikoff call. But as soon as Mona hung up with Becky the phone started ringing incessantly (over 900 times in less than two weeks),[1] and the house was surrounded by media.

Crews were at the street setting up their satellite links, reporters scattered on the lawn with their microphones and cameras. Black limousines and unmarked cars dotted the curbs. There were ABC, CBC, NBC, FOX, CNN and MSNBC reporters, all from the local media and most of the major national news outlets. Helicopters hovered above the house. Tom, after consulting with Brandon, received Mona's message and went straight to her house. He managed to fight past the cameras and microphones and make his way inside. He brokered a deal with the reporters that if Mona gave them a short statement they would promise to stay at the curb and out of the yard. Mona stepped outside and briefly said what would be the first public statement from the family to the world: "My husband is a good father and a good man and did not have anything to do with the Madrid Spain bombing, and we are praying for his early release." She hoped they would see the sincerity in her face and the truth behind her words, but it was hard to fight what the FBI alleged was Brandon's "100%" link to the attacks. She shut the door and went back in, overwhelmed by the outside crowd.

Tom was not overly optimistic but encouraged Mona to be patient and trust that justice would prevail—eventually. She listened half-heartedly as she pulled the curtains and blinds shut. The kids were peeking out at the reporters, shocked and afraid. Samir through tears mumbled, "This isn't our house. They took our dad, they took our things, and it doesn't feel like home anymore." Sharia turned on the television while looking on at those streaming the reports just yards away. When she saw her dad's face on every channel next to the horrifying images of the Madrid train bombings, her eyes welled up. She touched the image of his photo on the screen and whispered, "Poor dad, he never complained about anything and never hurt anyone, and look what happened to him." Mona walked into the living room, stepped in front of Sharia and turned off the television. "I don't want you watching any of this."

Later that night, Sharia heard a scratching sound inside her bedroom closet and cracked open the door to their meowing cats: Pooty and Pepsi. The FBI had locked the pets in the closet without food and water and did not bother to let them out upon leaving. Mona and the children were terrified. They could not sleep. The two younger ones climbed in bed with their mother and cried until they were shaking and their eyes dried up. Outside, the relentless media flashed floodlights through the window of the living room, broadcasting live news reports to the world. Helicopters still sounded in the distant sky, taking what must have been aerial photos of the house. Up in his room, Shane turned on the news and saw just how surrounded they were. Frequently, stadium lights at the curb were kicked on with a loud pop, and shined onto the reporters, casting a long, dark shadow. He would crack the blinds and see the back of a reporter in the yard while simultaneously watching the front of the same reporter on the television.

Mona had unplugged the telephone before retiring for the night; she could not deal with the terror that had struck her home and destroyed her family. She sleeplessly lay next to her children, worried about her husband. He had not contacted her all day, and there was no way of knowing when he would or if he could. She thought of him alone in a cold prison cell, an innocent man only to his family and close friends. Would the other inmates believe him? Did they even know who he was? How would they react? Sure, he had served in the army, but raising a family and working in a claustrophobic law office for years had softened him. Mona told herself to hold it together, to be strong for her children because they needed her. But who would be strong for Mona? Who would console her? She rolled onto her side, away from her children and silently cried. "So this is my first day of hell," she thought.

§ § §

[1] According to personal phone records.

Chapter 12
Lockdown

"The securest place is a prison cell, but there is no liberty."
Benjamin Franklin

L ater that evening, Brandon was escorted by guards to the cell where he would be imprisoned, up the elevator and down a long narrow corridor lit by dim fluorescent lights. Fatigued, he shuffled his plastic slippers and rattling chains across the floor.

The guards led him around the corner at the end of the hall where they radioed in for permission to enter. The bolts mechanically released, and the heavy steel doors clanged loudly as Brandon walked into Lock Down. The tiled area inside was triangular shaped, about the size of a living room, with tiny cells on one side, a single shower on the opposite side and a small room with blinds on the other. It was not until later that Brandon realized that the small room was the guard booth. The guards could crack the blinds and monitor the inmates at any moment.

One guard unlocked the steel door to the cell where Brandon would spend over a week in maximum security and full lock down. The cell was approximately 6 x 8 feet in size, with an aluminum toilet-sink unit by the door and steel bunk beds toward the back. There was a small double-pained steel-reinforced window just above the top bunk that looked out over the street below and across the Willamette River into East Portland. Brandon hesitated at the door, reluctant to enter his new abode.

It was approximately 10:00 P.M., and bemused inmates peered through the windows of their cell doors as the guards removed his chains. A new prisoner brought a rush of excitement to most of the faces of otherwise jaded and lifeless men. There was, however, one expressionless man in the next cell. Brandon locked eyes with him for a second before stepping into his own. The man was the most vocal on the floor and shouted profanities at whomever would listen. As the guard fiddled with his keys, one inmate yelled out to the guys in the cells next to Brandon, "Hey, here comes your buddy."

When the guards locked the cell door behind Brandon and left the floor, Brandon felt overwhelmingly lonely. He stood in the middle of his dark cell and raised his hands to his head, rubbing his temples. Sweat trickled down his back and under his arm pits even though it was cold. There was no way out. The vocal man in the cell to the left provoked the other inmates, threatening to bend them over and describing in graphic detail other equally offensive acts he would have them engage in. Brandon was uncertain if the remarks were addressed to anyone in particular or him specifically, but he was not comforted in either case knowing that the man and others like him were housed on the same floor. The other inmates cowered at the remarks, none brave enough to tell him what they all wished they could say. Eventually the floor became quiet, except for the occasional echo of a cough or the sound of someone snoring. When it went quiet it stayed quiet and no one dared disturb the silence.

Brandon's heart thudded and his stomach turned violently. He needed to use the toilet but was terrified of breaking the silence. He had not heard anyone else flushing or using the sink that late at night and agonized at the fate that might befall him if he were to wake anyone. Unaware of proper jail etiquette, and after weighing the pain of stomach cramps against the risk of waking someone, he decided he had to relieve himself.

When he was done, he sighed in relief that the others were still sleeping, or at least enough so not to yell at him. But he had no idea how to flush the thing. There were three buttons in total. One was for hot water, one for cold water, and one for flushing, but when he pressed the flush button nothing happened. He was unsure if he should have or even could have contacted anyone so he left it. Scared and tired, he crawled up to the top steel bunk onto a lumpy plastic mattress and spread out the blue prison blanket provided to him. With the smell of an unflushed toilet, and with serious criminal charges before him, he knew he was in a deep rut. He could not help but feel anger and despair at his situation. He looked out the window to the streets of Portland below where he had once walked a free man and winced at the thought of never walking them again.

It was there in that cold dark cell that he reflected on the gravity of the situation. A nightmare was unraveling before his eyes, as a flood of thoughts and questions raced through his head. He concluded after his brief visit earlier that Chris, the public defender, probably believed he was connected to the Spain bombing. Even though Chris did not say so explicitly, his expressions and tone made it clear. As an attorney, Brandon knew that in a best case scenario he would be released in the distant future. As long as the FBI insisted it had a 100% fingerprint match, he was going nowhere but into a downward spiral with a potentially fatal demise. In the worst case, he could be executed. It was the first time Brandon was forced to contemplate his own death. He did not want to die. He felt there was more he needed to do in life, more yet to accomplish and see. His oldest son was not even an adult yet.

As he thought about a possible life-time imprisonment or death, he wondered how his family would get along without him. When he had dropped Samir and Sharia off at school that morning he had promised them he would see them later that day, God willing. But he was not there to pick them up. They were counting on him to be there for them, and he never showed up. Brandon choked back tears. How would they manage without him in the days, weeks, and perhaps even years to come? He wanted to tell them he was okay, that he could handle whatever he had to endure, but he was not so sure of it.

Unable to sleep, he slid off the bunk and stood in the middle of the cell. He wondered what everyone else was thinking about the allegations. By then, he figured, anyone in the world who owned a television or a radio knew Brandon Mayfield had been arrested. Distant relatives back in Kansas and old friends who had not heard from him in years, some who probably did not even know he had become a Muslim, now "knew" he was a terrorist. He cringed at the legacy he would leave behind, at the fact that all the good he had ever done would be eclipsed by his descent into "terrorism."

Growing up in Kansas, Brandon's early life had not been easy. His dad spent many nights away drinking while his mom spent the days working as a high school art teacher. As a boy, Brandon had seen the rift grow between his parents, and any semblance of marital normalcy crumble before his naïve eyes. Though his parents were kind and loving on their own, it was impossible for them to forge a relationship when neither saw each other very often.

Brandon looked up to his dad who, despite only finishing high school, was articulate and intelligent. He was always there for him but was not always around. He taught Brandon and his two brothers how to harvest crops, fix cars, and mend fences. His dad, like Brandon and his brothers, had his occasional run in with the law but admonished them not to steal or lie.

After his arrest for the broken window, Brandon pushed himself outside his comfort zone and the Kansas borders that made up the home of his youth. He felt fortunate that he had come so far: he had a family, got an education, and served his country as a soldier. He did not drink like his dad but bore some of his father's characteristics, like an unmistakable Arcadian charm and Midwestern handiness. He had fixed up houses and made them homes, dedicating his spare time to minor indoor and major outdoor repairs. He liked to keep busy building, fixing, and mending things. If there was ever a problem he would find a solution.

But when he was brought before Judge Jones earlier in the day, he was met with a problem over which he had no control and could think of no immediate solution. He pled the best he could, something he was used to doing in the courtroom, except the stakes were much higher. He had pending cases filed in that very courthouse and had been there on a regular basis. He was a lawyer, an officer of the court. How could the judge believe the allegations? Officer of the court. He wore the title like a badge. But none of it mattered. For the time being he was a Muslim and nothing else.

He then thought of all the parallel lives he could have been living had he made just one different decision. He had left a law firm on the Oregon Coast, a place where he was fairly happy, shortly after 9/11. It was the first time he had practiced law since passing the bar, and though he was delayed in building his career due to serving in the army he was excited. Unfortunately, Newport, Oregon, was a small town of about 10,000 and the children were bored with the constant gray skies. Partly because he wanted his children to be around a more diverse group of people, especially fellow Muslims, and partly because he wanted his own office, Brandon moved to the Portland metro area. He faulted the move as the catalyst for his entire arrest. If he had lived a quiet, boring life in Newport, he probably would not have been implicated in this huge mess. He would not have mingled with other Muslims, as there were almost none, he would not have taken any controversial cases, and he never would have attended anti-war protests. Portland had politicized him too much and allowed him to flourish as a Muslim lawyer. That was exactly the thing you avoided if you feared intrusive government surveillance.

Brandon could not blame himself for his wrongful arrest, however. His deepest feeling was that somehow he was being framed, and that if there was a fingerprint involved perhaps it was forged. There was simply no other logical explanation. Could one fingerprint match alone, confirmed by FBI forensics specialists and coupled with circumstantial evidence gathered by the FBI, be enough to overcome the logistical impossibility that Brandon could have been in two places at once during the train bombings? That was precisely the fantastical reality before Brandon, who had been eating dinner at home on the night of the attack.

The loneliness Brandon felt in his cell was not just the feeling of being isolated from family and friends. It was the more nefarious possibility that his own government had betrayed him, targeted him, spied on him, falsely accused him, and left him alone to defend himself against impending death. Brandon, an all-American Muslim, felt like an alien in his own country. He crawled back in his bed but did not sleep. It was the longest, darkest night.

§ § §

America recently reached a new milestone, overtaking both Russia and Rwanda for "highest percentage of its citizens behind bars." [1] With a record 2.2 million incarcerated (nearly 1% of all adults), America's incarceration rates have increased by over 500% in the last forty years.[2] This is mostly due to changes in laws and policies and not necessarily to a marked increase in crime.[3] For example, the War on Drugs has led to over ten times as many people incarcerated for drug offenses than in 1980.[4]

There is a correlation between the number of laws that allow the investigation and prosecution of people and the number of people in prison as a result of those investigations. The expansion of the categories of crimes and classes of people punishable by imprisonment, the growth and privatization of prisons, and the lengthening of sentences through mandatory sentencing, have greatly contributed to the shocking 500 percent increase in the number of people in prison since 1972. Like the War on Drugs, the "War on Terror" has claimed scores of people, innocent and guilty alike. These wars have made crime prevention and combating terrorism profitable.

For example, while Dick Cheney was defense secretary, the Pentagon chose Halliburton subsidiary KBR to study whether they believed it was cost effective to outsource some military operations to private contractors. Based on the results of the study, the Pentagon hired KBR to implement the very outsourcing they recommended. Cheney later became Chief Executive Officer of Halliburton from 1995 through August 2000. The company's KBR subsidiary is the main government contractor working to restore Iraq's oil industry in an open-ended contract that was awarded without competitive bidding. Halliburton has reportedly been paid $10.7 billion for Iraq-related government work during 2003 and 2004.[5] KBR was also awarded a $30 million contract in July 2005 to build a 220-bed prison for terrorism suspects at Guantanamo Bay.[6]

Increasingly, private corporations are taking over our functions of government. KBR's involvement in prison construction and management is just part of a much wider trend of private for-profit domination of traditional government functions. In short, crime control, like waging wars, is big business.

§ § §

[1] "Trends in U.S. Corrections." The Sentencing Project. Web. 31 Aug. 2014. <http://sentencingproject.org/doc/publications/ inc_Trends_in_Corrections_Fact_sheet.pdf>

[2] *Id.* at 2.

[3] *Id.*

[4] *Id.* at 3.

[5] Fernandez, John S. "X Globalization and Security: The US 'Imperial Presidency': Global Impacts in Iraq and Mexico." John Saxe Fernández. 7 Aug. 2007. Web. 25 Sept. 2014. <http://jsaxef.blogspot.com/2007/08/ x-globalization-and-security-us.html>.

[6] "Halliburton Is Given New Prison Contract." The New York Times. The New York Times, 18 June 2005. Web. 25 Sept. 2014. <http:// www.nytimes.com/2005/06/19/politics/19gitmo.html?_r=0>.

Chapter 13
Trust in God, Family, and the Spanish Police

"Youth fades; love droops, the leaves of friendship fall; a mother's secret hope outlives them all." Oliver Wendell Holmes (1809-1894)

Mona spent the next three days not eating and buried her woes in cigarettes and coffee. The mosque Brandon attended was stormed by reporters and local Muslims were questioned. Everyone who knew him at the mosque was shocked that he would be involved in any kind of criminal act, but they were afraid. Mona noticed initially that many in the Muslim community were avoiding her.

The day after Brandon was arrested the children stayed home, and Mona contemplated pulling them from school one month before classes were scheduled to end. She was afraid for their safety. Not only were calls coming in from reporters, but hundreds of regular people were leaving voice messages at the home and office and sending hateful e-mails. However, not everyone was vitriolic; some even called to offer their support, both financially and emotionally. A family friend, a sweet and politically active woman, consoled Mona, told her she did not believe the allegations, and that she would be willing to help with expenses if necessary. One school counselor also called and ensured that safety parameters would be set up to promote a supportive learning environment. Mona considered taking her friend up on the gratuitous offer of financial aid. The only money the family had, secured in a safety deposit box, was seized by the FBI. It was inherited by Mona from her father after he had passed away when she was a child. Humiliated to immediately turn to friends and the Muslim community for help, she opted instead to ask only close family members for just enough money to pay the bills.

Brandon's mother and her partner flew in from Kansas on Saturday. Avnell, a graceful woman with long blond hair, blue eyes, and an eccentric, artsy fashion sense, left as soon as she could. When she arrived at the house there were between forty and fifty reporters. Brandon's brother Kent and his girlfriend Tonya also arrived shortly thereafter. With a house full of family and hearts full of fear, heads butted almost constantly.

§ § §

Sunday, Mother's day, was bittersweet for Brandon. It was the first time he had seen his family since the day of his arrest. Pained and from behind glass, he looked into the sleepless eyes of Mona and the worried eyes of his mother and knew, without speaking, that they were living their own hell. It was so hard to be just inches away and yet worlds apart. Mona explained how crazy the media was and how hard it was on her and the kids. Avnell offered comforting words of hope and encouraged Brandon to trust that everything would resolve itself. She was not religious but had a faith to her, always trusting that goodness would prevail. Brandon felt better knowing his mom and family were all together. Mona told Brandon she was praying a lot and urged Brandon to as well. He said he was, but did not explain the danger of performing so simple a deed. He asked her about the reaction from the Muslim community and she said they were noticeably quiet. Save for a few close friends most had not reached out at all, and she did not expect that they would.

Brandon felt sick. Some of his "friends" from the community, which he had dedicated much of his time and effort to be a part of, were too scared to rally in his support. He thought about the comment that the FBI agent made to him that the Muslims brothers would not be there for him like they were for Mike Hawash. The comment made sense for the first time. The Muslim community had stood with Hawash, and were so sure of his innocence that his later guilty plea had shocked and embarrassed them. Not again, they thought, embracing skepticism as their defense against similar future blunders. Now the FBI had an innocent man, and even the local Muslims were unsure of his innocence because of the claim of a 100% fingerprint match. Under the circumstances he could hardly blame them. Brandon felt he could rely only on very few. He reserved faith in God and trust in his family, true friends, and, oddly enough, the forensic expertise of the Spanish Police.

Chapter 14
Tea and Crumpets: Practicing Law
in Shackles and Chains

"The scattered tea goes with the leaves and every day a sunset dies."
William Faulkner

B y Monday Mona was having to contact clients and return retainers. When the FBI ransacked Brandon's office it confiscated numerous client files, interview notes, computer hard drives, pleadings, INS documents, phone logs, and just about every conceivable item that might contain a client confidence or secret. It is typically understood that, when clients come to an attorney, whatever they say is subject to a client-attorney privilege and will not be revealed except under very limited circumstances. The government in arresting and searching Brandon's home and office without probable cause not only violated Brandon's rights and privacy but that of his clients as well.

In an effort to downplay this particularly troubling and unethical aspect of its arrest, the FBI established a "taint" procedure using an Assistant United States Attorney, who was not a member of the prosecution's terrorism unit, to review the seized files for privileged and confidential material. Brandon objected to anyone looking at his client files under any circumstance. In response, the Public Defender moved for the immediate return of Brandon's files and their review by a special master. Judge Jones agreed and undertook the special master role himself. After reviewing the files in court and finding nothing suspicious, Judge Jones ordered the files released on Tuesday.

Brandon was unexpectedly called to a comfortable room in Judge Jones chambers as Federal Marshals sat watchfully in chairs just outside the door. Judge Jones turned his attention to Brandon and asked quietly so the marshals could not hear, "Can I offer you something to eat, a snack, some tea and crumpets perhaps?" Brandon could not recall the last time, if ever, he had been offered tea and crumpets but graciously accepted as he waited for his attorneys to arrive. When they did Judge Jones dropped several uncovered boxes on the top of the round conference table in the middle of the room. Brandon immediately recognized many of his legal files and briefs. Judge Jones explained the file review and told Brandon he could access the files and a phone if necessary, but only to discuss client matters.

Brandon looked dumbfounded at Chris and Steve. Essentially he was being asked to contact his clients and continue his practice the best he could while simultaneously being held in jail to fend for himself amongst the general prison population. Brandon asked Chris and Steve if they realized how awkward and ridiculous the situation was. They said they did, but not to complain because 1) it was probably preferable to being back in lockdown, and 2) it might give him an opportunity to let Judge Jones see he was human and not a criminal terrorist hell-bent on destruction. It did not take much convincing. Brandon decided that it was preferable sitting there in the climate-controlled judge's chambers sipping tea and dipping crumpets over watching his back every two minutes at the cell.

Chris and Steve left momentarily and Brandon began to look through a few of the files while eying the phone. He rehearsed what he would tell his clients. "Hello this is your attorney Brandon. As you know, I was arrested in connection with the Madrid Spain bombing and therefore may be tied up in jail for a little while as I hang out for a grand jury to convene. I can assure you I will do my upmost to continue to zealously represent you here in jail, but unfortunately I may not be able to take your calls, appear on your behalf in court, do legal research, or meet with you in person except behind glass after being subjected to a full cavity search." And, "Oh yea, don't worry about me voluntarily revealing any of your most confidential information and any secrets you may have shared with me in the course of our legal relationship. The government has already gone over all our notes and files with a fine tooth comb, so there's probably little more I could share that they have not already discovered."

Chris and Steve returned to the room. They could hear some noise in the next room, raised but muffled voices. It was Judge Jones admonishing the Assistant U.S. attorney regarding the leaks from the government in violation of Judge Jones' gag orders. Even while the government had strict orders not to reveal any information about the details of the material witness proceedings, leaks were flowing like a sieve both locally and back in Washington.

Brandon's short-lived respite practicing law was brought to a sobering end when he finally had to return to the detention center. Every time Brandon was moved to and from the Federal Courthouse he was ushered to various holding cells. Sometimes he would be in the same area as incoming inmates being processed. Some of the other inmates knew who he was, some did not. He was probably more concerned for his physical safety in the holding cell than in any other place. The wait could be over an hour, and three to seven other people were crammed in the cell together with no guards. Brandon had been in the army, had been charged with defending his country. Yet being alone in a holding cell with up to a dozen potentially hardened criminals was a scarier, more intimate confrontation with violence.

Once, while in the holding cell, Brandon listened half-heartedly to the casual gossip until something spiked his attention. A younger guy with long hair and a short black goatee and a slight white guy with a rough composure asked a question. "You all know about that fuck, Ward Weaver, yeah?" Ward Weaver was a well-known accused sex offender and murderer. The three other people nodded and one chimed in.

"Oh yeah, he'll get what's comin' to 'im alright."

"Well, I heard he was put in the medical ward in a facility not too far away," the rough guy said and cracked a morbid smile. "It'd be real easy to slip past security there, and perform a laying on of hands for him."

"People like that, they don't deserve to live," one said.

Brandon did not speak a word. He retreated to a corner of the room and looked on at the men before him who were beaming at the thought of vigilante justice, prison style. He felt vulnerable and unsafe. If an alleged murderer was enough to incite the rage of inmates, how would they react to the presence of an alleged terrorist in the very room they were in? A terrorist mastermind behind the deadliest attacks since 9/11? Brandon hoped they would not recognize him, but he knew that as the weeks passed it would be inevitable.

Every day he lived was a miracle, he thought. With the frequent, but brief, interaction with multitudes of incensed, and sometimes crazy or detoxing inmates, it was shocking he was still alive. Still, he was more afraid of the government than the inmates. Steve had informed him that there was a risk he could be transferred to Guantanamo Bay or a military prison as an enemy combatant. Brandon did not want to even think about how people were treated, or rather tortured, there.

§ § §

Just days after the September 11 attacks, Congress passed a resolution known as the Authorization for Use of Military Force which gave the president sweeping powers to label any person he chose as being involved in the terrorist attacks. There was no guidance or oversight in its grant of authority. The AUMF stated:

> "That the President is authorized to use all necessary and appropriate force against those nations, organizations, or persons he determines planned, authorized, committed, or aided the terrorist attacks that occurred on September 11, 2001, or harbored such organizations or persons, in order to prevent any future acts of international terrorism against the United States by such nations, organizations or persons." [1]

Not fully satisfied with the broad powers granted by Congress, on November 13, 2001, the Bush Administration issued a Presidential Military Order entitled the "Detention, Treatment, and Trial of Certain Non-Citizens in the War Against Terrorism." It allowed "individuals...to be detained, and when tried, to be tried for violations of the laws of war and other applicable laws by military tribunals," where such individuals are members of al-Qaeda or have conspired or committed acts of international terrorism, or have as their aim to cause injury to or adverse effects on the United States, its citizens, national security, foreign policy, or economy.[2] This gave the president and his staff the ability to label anyone they chose an enemy combatant and subject them to detention indefinitely without a trial—military or otherwise.

Yasir Hamdi, amongst the first of Guantanamo Bay's detainees, was captured in Afghanistan in 2001 and labeled an enemy combatant.[3] When it became known that he was a U.S. citizen, he was transferred to jails in Virginia and South Carolina.[4] Hamdi challenged his detention. On June 28, 2004, the

Supreme Court repudiated the government's assertion of executive authority to suspend the constitutional protections afforded to U.S. citizens. The court warned that a "state of war is not a blank check for the President when it comes to the rights of the Nation's Citizens." [5] The opinion of the Court did not preclude citizen-detainees from receiving military tribunals; rather, the tribunals in such instances were considered lawful so long as the detainee could question his enemy combatant status before a neutral decision-maker. The neutral decision-maker need not be a judge. Moreover, hearsay would be allowed, and the burden of proof would shift to the defendant. These changes, seemingly minor, are a significant departure from the procedural due process that citizens in U.S. criminal courts generally receive.

Later cases would further elucidate the extent to which the government was authorized to hold a citizen indefinitely without the right to counsel, the writ of habeas corpus, or notice of charges. However, in May, 2004, just a month before the Supreme Court ruled in the *Hamdi* case, nothing was certain. Brandon had no assurance that he would stay in Oregon. He frequently worried that he would be labeled an enemy combatant by the Executive Branch and sent to Guantanamo Bay, with no right to speak with counsel or be heard before a judge. He could be held indefinitely and tortured. He would be presumed guilty. And if there was any process it would likely be in a much-dreaded military tribunal.

§ § §

[1] See "Joint Resolution." GPO. Web. 4 Sept. 2014.< http://www.gpo.gov/ fdsys/pkg/PLAW-107publ40/html/PLAW-107publ40.htm> for text>

[2] "Military Order of November 13, 2001 -- Detention, Treatment, and Trial of Certain Non-Citizens in the War Against Terrorism." FAS. 13 Nov. 2001. Web. 4 Sept. 2014. <http://fas.org/irp/offdocs/eo/mo-111301.htm>. [Federal Register: November 16, 2001 (Volume 66, Number 222) Presidential Documents Page 57831-57836].

[3] Schmitz, Charles. "Beating a Slow, Stubborn Retreat at Guantanamo Bay | Middle East Research and Information Project." Middle East Research and Information Project. 1 May 2014. Web. 5 Sept. 2014. <http://

www.merip.org/mero/interventions/beating-slow-stubborn-retreat-guantanamo-bay>.

4 *Id.*

5 Hamdi v. Rumsfeld 542 U.S. 507 (2004). For text, see "Hamdi v. Rumsfield, 542 U.S. 507 (2004)." U.S. Civil Liberties. 7 Sept. 2012. Web. 5 Sept. 2014. <http://uscivilliberties.org/cases/3898-hamdi-v-rumsfield-542-us-507-2004.html>.

Chapter 15
Darkness and Despair

"It's so much darker when a light goes out than it would have been if it had never shone." John Steinbeck, *The Winter of Our Discontent*

Brandon was escorted along with several other cell mates from lock down towards the visitation area. While in the hall, he was accosted by apprehensive guards.

"Hey! We're going to have to search you," a guard said and immediately ran his hands up and down the blue uniform. "You have anything in your pockets?"

"Just some tissue," Brandon answered. The man pulled out the crumpled toilet paper, dropped it to the ground and then kicked it to the side.

"Okay, you're good," he said, breathing on Brandon's face and nudging him along. Brandon jerked forward and made nothing of the search.

Later, while waiting in the visiting booth, Brandon felt something unfamiliar in his pocket and pulled out a small tan packet, slightly resembling a tea bag. Horrified and unsure what it was, he let it fall to the floor with the inconspicuousness of a casual litterer. Was it some sort of message? Did the guards put it there to frame him? Brandon wondered what would have happened if he were to have been searched again and caught having "lied" about having nothing in his pocket. One thing was sure: someone was out to get him, but who and why he did not know. From that moment on he was just as distrusting of the guards as he was the inmates.

Kent arrived in the visiting area with shoulder length hair pulled back in a pony-tail, and Shane's normal toughness was replaced with a long, sad face. Brandon was surprised to see them both, especially his brother who had aged since the last time they had met. After brief hellos and suppressed disbelief at the ludicrousness of the entire situation, Kent confided to Brandon.

"I asked Chris and Steve what they thought about this all, and Chris said he believed you were innocent. Steve did not answer one way or the other.

But I want you to know we all believe in you and that you'll get out of here. Just stay strong." Brandon appreciated the encouragement but swallowed his own apprehension, knowing better about the bleak future before him.

"You guys too. I want you to stay strong, especially you Shane. You're the oldest and the kids look up to you. I want you guys to take care of yourselves." Brandon felt helpless as a father, pained that his incarceration caused his family so much distress.

Shane fought back tears as he peered at his confined father through the glass. A silence befell the three of them and Shane's chest heaved and tears streaked his cheeks.

"How are you holding up? How are things at home? In school?" Brandon asked.

"Fine dad," he managed to say between choked sobs. "Fine. I'm not going to school. They gave me the option to sit out." He looked away from his dad, ashamed. Shane was a quiet intellectual and had, until then, gotten good grades without ever trying. From a young age he was perceptive and had a knack for history. When Shane was just a child, Brandon would quiz him about historical events such as the major wars and the fall of the Roman Empire, as well as geography such as the location of the Ganges and Yangtze rivers and the seven wonders. Shane marveled at the world and had acquired a global consciousness. When his siblings were old enough, Brandon made up a "board game" called the "Key of Wisdom." Each of the three kids would start by standing on a linoleum kitchen tile. Brandon would ask them questions based on their intelligence level, and every correct answer allowed the kid to move to the next tile. The goal was to make it across the kitchen first, strategize to block off the others, and increase one's knowledge. The winner was given the key of wisdom, a cardboard skeleton key that symbolized mental prowess and knowledge. Shane, fiercely competitive, almost always won and had carried on his zeal to school. But since his dad's arrest, he had no passion for learning. All of it seemed trivial compared to the impending fate his dad faced. His grades dropped and would continue to drop even long after his dad's ordeal.

"What about dragon boating?" Brandon asked, already knowing the answer.

"Nothing. I'm doing nothing now," Shane answered.

"Look, I want you to go to school, okay? And keep rowing. Please, do it for me. It'll get your mind off things. It's a good way to relax," Brandon explained.

"Okay, dad." Shane answered, unconvincingly.

"Shane, I mean it. You need to go to school and keep rowing. Keep rowing, okay?" Brandon's voice quivered and he could not insist on the last point enough. He could not tell Shane the real reason he wanted him to keep rowing.

In Portland there is a Rose festival parade every summer down on the waterfront. Various rowers, including high school teams, race each other on the Willamette River. Each team consists of approximately ten paddlers to a boat. The boats look like large canoes covered in colorful ornate designs, such as red dragons, with other oriental characters sculptured on the front. From Brandon's jail cell window he was able to see the boats at the staging area of the river practicing for the upcoming races. The view of the river boardwalk, of freedom and leisure just beyond his reach, made the confinement all the more painful. He wanted desperately to tell Shane how important it was for him to continue rowing, but he feared the guards would hear and move him for security reasons or just out of spite. Each day, Brandon peeked out of his window hoping his son was out there, but it made no difference. Shane never went back and Brandon was later moved to a different floor without the same view.

§ § §

The Grand Jury was to convene on Friday, July 21st. Brandon's lawyers had told him of his two options: either he would plead the 5th and risk being held in contempt of the court, or he would talk and risk indictment and possible perjury. There was no arguing with a "100%" fingerprint match. None of his options appealed to him. Brandon thought about what Kent had said to Steve and questioned him personally. He figured if he was going to face a possible protracted trial it would be helpful to know he had the trust and support of his attorneys.

"Well, do you think I'm innocent?" Brandon asked Steve.

"Brandon, I don't even think about that, and I don't get into that," Steve answered plainly. At the time it hurt Brandon. It was important that if he was going to be charged and possibly convicted of something he did not do that at least his own attorney believed in him. But Brandon accepted it and understood. Even if Steve's faith in Brandon's innocence was still up in the air, his commitment to the case clearly was not. Together with the investigators at the Public Defender's office, Steve worked diligently and tirelessly, around the clock, to get to the bottom of the mystery of what was fast becoming the infamous Latent Print No. 17.

Meanwhile, Mona was frustrated and kept asking the Public Defender for information. She spoke mostly with Chris Schatz, who kept telling her there was a gag order and that he couldn't tell her anything except that Brandon was potentially facing a capital offense. Mona was not satisfied with being left in the dark.

"Chris, we're such boring people. All we did was go to the office, go to work, go to school, go home, and go to the kids' sports events. We don't have a special life. We don't have a fancy life. We're just getting by. Everything is just very simple and just kind of a one step at a time type of life."

Mona insisted her husband was innocent so vehemently Chris had begun to believe her. He admitted, "Yes, I think he's innocent, but you have to assume the worst. We're going to proceed presuming that the fingerprint is his." He continued, "Sometimes bad things happen to good people and there's enough evidence to indict him. There's a 100% match."

Mona said, "Well, then, we'll just go to trial."

Chris warned her, "You don't know that he'll be found innocent. You don't know what the government has. They can produce an informant that lies." When Mona heard those words she nearly lost it. Chris kept talking about going forward under the presumption there was a 100% match and trying to construct alibis or explanations for it. It was the logical tactic for an attorney. No lawyer would contest three forensics experts' consistent findings that LFP 17 and that of Brandon's left index finger were the same. But Mona and the family knew that the mark of foul play (or at the very least, careless work) was stamped all over the FBI's documents.

Mona became overwhelmed with the situation and did not know how to deal with the possibility of a capital offense and a lying informant. When

Chris came to the law office to inventory some of the things and take some pictures, Mona yelled at him in despair. "You need to tell me what to do here. I've got the office, I've got kids, I've got clients—do I need to close up shop here?" She then put her head down on the desk and cried. Her hope was waning each passing day as the possibility of Brandon's release was becoming more and more remote.

Chapter 16
The Awadallah Predicament

"I know it is warrantable by the law of God, and I think by the law of the land, that I may stand on my just defense, and not answer your interrogatories, and that my accusers ought to be brought face to face, to justify what they accuse me of." John Lilburne, 1638.
Precursor to 5th Amendment.

Steve and Chris quickly arranged a meeting with Judge Jones and the local U.S. attorneys to discuss when a grand jury might convene for Brandon to testify, unless he invoked his 5th amendment right to remain silent and not incriminate himself. Brandon wanted to be released as soon as possible, but depending on the outcome of the material witness proceeding he could face indictment for capital offenses and even perjury. Brandon carefully read the Awadallah opinion that the judge had handed him at his first appearance and understood the warning: testify at your own risk, knowing that the prosecution will likely charge you with perjury based on any inconsistent or forgetful statements you provide them or the grand jury after hours of grueling testimony.

Awadallah, a Jordanian immigrant, had the misfortune of writing about one of the would-be 9/11 hijackers in his college exam booklet.[1] Later, when questioned by the FBI, he could not recall the fact. The FBI, presumably having retained the booklet, was dissatisfied with his response. Awadallah corrected his testimony five days later, but the government, realizing he was not involved in the attacks in any way, chose instead to charge him with providing false statements[2]—an offense that carries a sentence of up to ten years in prison.

In 2002, Judge Scheindlin dismissed all the charges against Awadallah, ruling that the government had violated the Constitution by improperly using the material witness statute to jail witnesses for their terror probe.[3] The government appealed the decision and the 2nd Circuit Court of Appeals overturned Scheindlin and reinstated the charges.[4] The government was unable to get Judge Scheindlin removed on claims of bias[5] and tried Awadallah to a deadlocked trial in 2007, earning him a narrow acquittal.[6]

Brandon faced the same dilemma—the government feigned its only interest was in acquiring evidence from Brandon, but instead paraded him as a criminal defendant and primary suspect. If he appeared before the grand jury and invoked his Fifth Amendment right, the government could do one of two things: either grant him full immunity from prosecution and release him (very improbable) or else indict him. It was an impossible situation.

Given the possible capital consequences he was facing, exposure to a grand jury was extremely risky. Although he was a lawyer, he was not a criminal defense attorney, and his level of stress and lack of food and sleep were wearing him down. Chris and Steve explained that in addition to a possible indictment, if he invoked his Fifth Amendment right not to talk, he would be subject to a contempt citation and imprisonment for up to 18 months. They also informed him of the international implications and multi-jurisdictional issues peculiar to his unique situation. The "good" news was that, if implicated on charges of involvement in Spain and extradited, there was no chance of death penalty there; the bad news was that Spain would not honor any immunity the U.S. government might afford him in exchange for testimony. Even if it did, Brandon still faced possible prosecution in Spain if turned over.

Brandon, in a meeting with Chris asked him point blank, "Do you really think they can indict me?"

Chris answered sarcastically, "Brandon, they could indict a ham sandwich."

"But I had nothing to do with it! I think I should plead the fifth to avoid a possible perjury trap like they got Awadallah for. Then we can force them to indict me and prepare for trial." Brandon could see this kind of talk got Chris nervous. At first he wasn't sure if Chris thought he was guilty of involvement in Spain, but after a week in the detention center, Brandon could sense Chris did not doubt his innocence.

"You know the government can use paid witnesses who are often facing criminal charges of their own," Chris opined.

"So what if they are facing criminal charges?"

"I mean, these witnesses might testify against you in return for favorable plea agreements, reduced charges, or even cash. If they do indict you, I assure you, you'll remain in custody and there will be no trial for at least a year and a half minimum." Brandon had no idea what he was up against or why he was the target of what he thought was a clear framing. Was Chris implying that witnesses could testify falsely against him? How would Brandon defend against that? It was fantastical to him that his own country, the very one he risked his life to defend, was now the one he was defending his life against. The more he learned, the more helpless he felt.

Chris turned his attention to the bag. "Is it possible a client may have come into your office and your hand touched a blue plastic bag?" Chris asked.

"No, I would have remembered."

"Perhaps you were at someone else's house grabbing for a hand towel and you touched a blue plastic bag," Chris suggested. Brandon thought back to all the friends he visited and places he had been. "I don't think so." There was no explanation for how his fingerprint was on a bag full of detonators thousands of miles away. "Chris, I'm telling you, that fingerprint is not mine."

"But Brandon, we have to assume that it is," Chris answered cautiously.

"No, it is not my fingerprint and you have to assume that it's not my fingerprint," Brandon retorted.

"Then what other explanation can there be?" asked Chris.

"You cannot rule out the possibility of a mistake or foul play." Brandon was a bit shocked that Chris could entertain the idea of witnesses falsely testifying but not that the FBI had forged the "forensics" of the fingerprint match.

"What do you mean? You were framed?" Chris scoffed.

"Look," Brandon said. "This happened overseas, intelligence agencies or operatives from other countries could be involved in a variety of ways for a variety of reasons."

Chris paused for a moment, unmoved, and then said, "Do you think for a moment if such a well-planned job to frame you was orchestrated that we or anyone else could do anything for you?" The point was both sobering and terrifying.

Shortly after this conversation with Chris, Brandon was informed of even more disturbing news: the U.S. attorneys had just informed them that they had enough evidence to indict him, but not enough to convict him yet. The clock was ticking.

§ § §

[1] Hirschkorn, Phil. "Judge: Arrest of Sept. 11 witness was illegal." CNN. Cable News Network, 30 Apr. 2002. Web. 31 Aug. 2014. <http://edition.cnn.com/2002/LAW/04/30/perjury.dismissal/index.html?related>.

[2] *Id.*

[3] *Id.*

[4] Preston, Julia. "Trial Starts for Man Who Knew Hijackers." The New York Times. 19 Apr. 2006. Web. 25 Sept. 2014. <http://www.nytimes.com/2006/04/20/nyregion/20material.html?pagewanted=print>.

[5] *Id.*

[6] See United States v. Awadallah, 349 F3d 42 (2003).

Chapter 17
Soon This Too Shall Pass

"And never give up hope of God's soothing mercy: Truly no one despairs of God's soothing mercy except those who have no faith." Koran 12:87

Sulking in a small prison cell with nothing but dark walls to swallow him up, Brandon's mind wandered. It wandered into territories of his consciousness he never knew existed. It was in this freedom of thought that he faced the most horrifying of thoughts. Of his past, his present, and a bleak future. Of life and death. All the days were blending together, punctuated only by occasional sleep and visitations. He did not want to die like that: locked up, innocent, and as a terrorist in the eyes of the world. Brandon gripped his Koran tightly in his hand and then silently pled to God to give him a sign, some direction, some spiritual peace to replace his inner angst and tumult. He flipped open the book to a random page and told himself that whichever passage it opened to might hold a special message for him. He did this for three consecutive nights and carefully noted each one. On the first night he opened it to the middle of Chapter 13, Al Rad (The Thunder), and began to read:

"Say: Do you take for worship protectors other than him, such as have no power either for good or for harm to themselves? Say: Are the blind equal with those who see? Or the depths of darkness equal with Light?"

He then read the next page.

"Once God wills a people's punishment, there can be no turning it back, nor will they find, besides him, any to protect. It is he who doth show you the lightening, by way both of fear and hope. It is he who raises up the clouds, heavy with fertilizing rain.

"Nay, thunder repeats his praises and so do the angels with awe, he flings the loud voiced Thunderbolts, and therewith strikes whomsoever he will...Yet these are the men who dare to dispute about God, with the strength of His power Supreme."

Brandon was so shaken and disoriented from his confinement that by the time he finished the short chapter he realized he had read it backwards. Korans, true to the Arabic language, are usually translated from right to left, and Brandon was accustomed to reading them that way. However, the one the chaplain had given him was oriented in a more conventional, English way, from left to right. No matter, the message was clear. When God chose to administer a punishment there was nothing anyone could do in the slightest to change it. For the first time, Brandon began the process of accepting his fate.

The following evening, alone in his cell, Brandon again randomly opened the Koran. This time he came to the very beginning of Chapter 11, Hud (the prophet Hud). The chapter describes the fate of past generations and the various punishments they were met with as a result of their many inequities and sins. It includes the familiar stories of Noah and Lot, and of some less familiar prophets, such as Hud, who warned his community to mend their evil ways or else suffer God's punishment:

"They who hinder men from the path of God and would seek in it something crooked: these were they who denied the hereafter. They will in no way frustrate his design on earth nor have they protectors besides God! Their penalties will be doubled! They lost the power to hear and they did not see!"

Brandon continued.

"And establish regular prayers at the two ends of the day and at the approaches of the night: For those things that are good remove those that are evil: In that is remembrance to those who remember their Lord. And be steadfast in patience for verily God will not suffer the reward of the righteous to perish...

"Nor would thy Lord be the one to destroy communities for a single wrongdoing if its members were likely to mend."

Brandon thought about this verse in the context of his own community and country and wondered what their collective fate was. He wondered if there was enough good in society for its continued existence or would it, like all the empires of past, fall at God's command. Was fire and brimstone, flood and pestilence, certain? Would there be a natural disaster or world war? He also struggled to define community. Was it his city, state, country? Was it a more global religious community of all Muslims? He again prayed his evening prayer and decided to pray an afternoon prayer the following day in his cell, not just for him but for all the innocent people of the world who were suffering.

The next day, Brandon opened his Koran for the third time, again at random, and found himself at the beginning of Chapter 12, Yusuf (Joseph). Brandon read the beautiful story from start to finish. How Joseph was given the power to interpret dreams but was left to die in a well by his jealous brothers. How he was taken to Egypt by traveling merchants who found him in the well, only to be imprisoned wrongfully when the wife of the nobleman he worked for falsely accused him of attempting to rape her (after he rejected her desperate advances). How the King of Egypt learned of Joseph's gift for interpreting dreams and called upon him for his counsel. How he was exonerated of the false charges against him and offered a noble title. How he by chance was able to confront and later forgive the brothers who sought to harm him. How he invited everyone, including his parents, to come live with him in prosperity in Egypt. And how he said, at last:

"Oh my Lord! You have indeed bestowed on me some power, and taught me something of the interpretation of dreams and events— Oh creator of the heavens and the earth! You are my protector in this world and the hereafter. Take my soul at death as one submitting to thy will as a Muslim, and unite me with the righteous."

This story of mercy and hope, tucked away like a jewel between the preceding and following verses of foreboding and admonition, was the most beautiful and comforting story Brandon had ever read, at a time he could not have needed it more. Brandon lay down for the first time in the cooler bottom bunk, the burden on his heart just ever so slightly eased. He ruminated on the story of Joseph and the virtue of patience and faith in the face of adversity. As he looked up at the underside of the top bunk, he noticed in heavy pencil, for the first time, a message some distraught soul before him had scribbled. There in big dark letters were scratched the words "SOON THIS TOO SHALL PASS." Brandon smiled and for the first time a small flicker of hope lit up.

Chapter 18
Moses Will Tell the Truth

"Everything we hear is an opinion, not a fact. Everything we see is a perspective, not the truth." Marcus Aurelius

On Tuesday, May 18th, Brandon had been detained for close to two weeks. Most days were uneventful, but today he would go to court. As he stepped out of the van into the parking structure outside the courthouse, he thought back to his first day there in shackles. It seemed as though he had lived an entire life since then. He had first digested his fate, then contemplated it, then fought it, then accepted it. There was nothing left to do but wait and pray for strength to endure it. Fumbling over his leg chains, Brandon caught his foot on the metal step of the van and fell forward, catching himself with his face inches above the ground. With the hand cuffs running through the belly chain there was no way to protect the face, and the fall was only broken when his hands hit first. Brandon felt his left shoulder and wrist shoot with pain, as he struggled to regain composure and stand up. He looked up, defeated, at an unsympathetic marshal chuckling and shaking his head condescendingly.

§ § §

Because Brandon insisted that the fingerprint was not his, the Public Defender's office filed a motion requesting that a copy of the fingerprint in the FBI's possession be turned over to them so they could have it reviewed by an independent expert to assess if it was in fact his. Judge Jones had ruled on the motion and called the parties to address the issue for an afternoon hearing. Brandon was escorted into the courtroom before Judge Jones had arrived. After the judge entered everyone, including Brandon, stood up. Before proceeding, however, Judge Jones asked if the defendant was still in chains and if he had been given any lunch. Brandon answered that he was still in chains and that he had not been given any food during the transfer. The U.S. marshals looked embarrassed that they had not removed the shackles before his appearance or provided him anything to eat. Behind the counsel table, the judge would never know Brandon was in chains unless he moved about the courtroom. Brandon was glad to have the chains and shackles that were cutting into his ankles taken off and that the judge knew how weak he must have been from lack of food and sleep.

Judge Jones then proceeded. "Good Afternoon. In respect to this matter, the issue most pressing before the court is production of the fingerprint, which I ordered yesterday. I now understand that the fingerprint is available on disk and CD, and I will turn it over to the defense on these conditions. First of all, the fingerprint must be kept absolutely confidential."

The U.S. attorney immediately jumped in and objected to turning over the fingerprint image the FBI used to make its identification. He said if they were ordered to produce it, "My suggestion would be, rather than have us turn the fingerprint over to the defense, that we provide it to whichever expert the court selects. If it is Mr. Moses that the court selects, that's fine. We will get it to him and go forward from there."

The judge then asked the prosecutor a question referring to the proposed fingerprint examiner's findings. "What would happen if he reports to the court that it is a perfect match? Could the government then call him as a witness if there is an indictment against the material witness?" Brandon was anxious to hear the government's reply.

The U.S. attorney for the prosecution paused for a moment, thought about the question, and replied deliberately. "I guess we would like to do that. If for some reason the FBI lab's competency is questioned, my inclination is to call the FBI folks. That's their job." The government was very insistent on not turning over the fingerprint evidence directly to the Public Defender and only to a court-appointed expert of their approval. The U.S. attorney continued anxiously, "I will say this, your Honor; if it is critical to your decision, we would be willing to give up the right to call him as a witness down the road if it is a positive match." Judge Jones took them up on the offer and clarified that so long as "your agreement is that the court can send this to Mr. Moses to do his own testing, and that irrespective of the results he could not be called as a witness against the accused."

Chris, Steve, and Brandon stepped outside of the courtroom to discuss the proposal. Steve explained that it was rare to get any review of evidence in a material witness proceeding so they were fortunate. He said that Mr. Moses was not their favorite pick, but they had nothing to lose as long as he could not be called as a witness against Brandon if the government were to indict. Brandon told Steve that he knew it was not his fingerprint and if an expert, who was not connected to the FBI, examined it they would also conclude it was not his. Brandon qualified that he was in agreement only so long as the FBI had absolutely no contact with Mr. Moses so as to not taint the procedure.

When they went back into the courtroom, the government was already waiting to poison the well. While the judge dictated the order for the government to turn over the fingerprint to Mr. Moses, the U.S. attorney calculated his next request. In the politest voice he could muster, he asked, "Your honor, while we are waiting, can I ask," he paused, "can we have our FBI lab people talk to him also just so they can explain what they have done or answer his questions?" Brandon was furious at the request, but Judge Jones agreed and suggested the FBI's chief examiner be allowed to talk directly to Moses. Brandon shook his head, waiting for Steve to respond. Fortunately, he did.

"Your honor, our concern there is the potential for tainting the independence of his examination and the potential for the communication by the FBI to be putting some pressure on him."

Judge Jones met in the middle and modified the order, allowing Mr. Moses to contact the FBI's chief examiner to fully discuss the issue but not for the FBI to contact him. Brandon was disappointed, because he knew that with that permission, given the notoriety the disputed fingerprint was causing, that Moses would feel compelled to consult. Brandon had no other alternative and could only hope that Mr. Moses' analysis was truly independent and accurate (assuming he was being provided a true copy of the latent print found on the bag in Spain) and not swayed or pressured by the FBI's "methodology."

One of the Public Defender's top investigators, an English barrister, was tasked with flying a copy of the digital image fingerprint cards on the first flight from Portland to San Francisco. There, Mr. Moses would examine the prints and report to the court via teleconferencing the following day, immediately following his finding. This was Brandon's first opportunity to challenge the government's assurance that they had identified his fingerprints on the bag from Madrid. Before he was escorted back to his cell, Brandon asked Steve what would happen if Moses did conclude the fingerprint was his. He answered honestly, "Brandon, if that happens, there is a good chance they will indict you on criminal charges."

§ § §

The very next morning, Brandon was hauled back up to the 10th floor of the courthouse where everyone in the courtroom was on pins and needles—including the court staff and the U.S. marshals in the dark recesses of the wings—waiting anxiously to hear from Mr. Moses. The court clerk fiddled around with her equipment and finally managed to get a good line with Mr. Moses. "Mr. Moses, can you hear me?" she said.

The Judge repeated, "Mr. Moses?"

Finally from the other side, the voice of Moses sounded, "Yes."

Judge Jones continued. "We are ready to proceed. Will you raise your right hand and take this oath." The oath was read.

"I do," said Moses.

"In a nutshell, can you tell me what your ultimate conclusion is as to whether this fingerprint can be identified as that of Mr. Mayfield?" Judge Jones asked.

Moses said very clearly and distinctly, "Yes. I compared the latent prints to the known prints that were submitted on Brandon Mayfield, and I concluded that the latent print is the left index finger of Mr. Mayfield."

Brandon was stunned but remained stone-faced. At first, he wanted to jump from his seat and yell at Mr. Moses to examine his middle finger, but knew such indignations were pointless at best and incriminating at worst. But his anger soon turned to despair and then sorrow. Brandon wondered what forces were conspiring against him and if the judge would ever believe him now. Moses was supposed to be the silver lining, the voice of reason and truth—but even he had been "persuaded." Brandon felt that the life he once knew was over for good and fought back the tears that were too proud to rear themselves on his sullen face. He would not give them the satisfaction that they had defeated him. He would fight the injustice and cloak his devastation in valiant protest. Brandon glanced over at Chris and Steve who were also visibly stunned. Only moments before, they were upbeat and jubilant, smiling and confident in anticipation of good news. Now they were totally slumped in their chairs, faces long and skeptical. They were floored by Moses' findings.

Chris Schatz managed to pick himself up out of his chair and briefly crossed Moses about the identification. "Mr. Moses, was this a difficult comparison to make in your opinion?"

Moses admitted as much, especially without the original. "Yes, it was quite difficult. My best opinion is that the image was developed with cyanoacrylic fuming, which is the same as super glue fuming, which is commonly used on plastics. There is some distortion and some blotting out by the cyanoacrylate residue, but there is still ample image to evaluate."

Chris quickly finished his exam with a final question. "To reach an ultimate determination of authenticity concerning the latent print, would it be important to have access to the original print?"

Mr. Moses answered honestly, "Yes. I always like to examine the original because there are things you can tell from the surface and the texture and substrate that you cannot tell from the photograph. It is always useful in examining the potentiality of fraud or some faking of a fingerprint."

The judge thanked Mr. Moses and disconnected him. Brandon's lifeline faded off the screen, the pixels went black, and with that Brandon's hope for release completely died. Judge Jones then addressed the government. "You have a matter you wanted to discuss in open court with counsel."

"Yes, your honor, just briefly," replied The U.S. attorney. "I advised the court that we had received some information from Spain this morning that casts some doubt on the fingerprint identification. We are in the process of trying to run that down. I think it will take a couple of days to do that." Chris, Steve, and Brandon looked at the U.S. attorneys, puzzled by the sudden revelation. It was overwhelmingly good news.

The U.S. attorney continued, "The matter, as I understand right now, is either classified or potentially classified. So I am not at liberty to discuss it further in this setting. I would be happy to tell the Court in chamber because you do have a clearance. We are doing our best to get the matter declassified and, as I say, run it down."

Judge Jones responded, "Well in respect to that, I will need to know the seriousness of the matter at this point. I don't know if we are talking about something that would totally render the fingerprint unreliable as far as where it was found and so forth. Because it might well require some action in respect to the motion for release, I will need to talk to you in chamber with respect to that...I will meet with counsel in my conference room, with the government off the record. If you will wait, it will be a few moments." Judge Jones glanced over at a dumbfounded Steve, Chris, and Brandon.

While the government and the judge were meeting in secret, Chris, Steve, Brandon, and the Public Defender's investigator were allowed the jury room to discuss the matter. After shuffling into the room, Brandon asked in disbelief, "Did the government just say that they have something that puts the fingerprint identification in doubt?"

Chris said, "Yeah, he did say the identification is potentially in doubt, right?" No one could believe their ears.

Steve affirmed, "Yes. But why would it be deemed classified? Does Judge Jones even have a security clearance to hear classified information?"

"I am not sure," Chris shrugged.

"Surely he must have it," Brandon said, "considering the type of cases he hears, including terrorism cases."

Steve replied, "Why couldn't they share it with us if it's only classified? How and who classifies this information?" Even the head honcho Public Defender's office with over 20 years of experience was stumped. It was surreal.

Brandon thought about his question and asked Chris and Steve, "You guys at the Public Defender's office all have secret clearances, right?"

They looked at him in amusement and shook their heads no. "No, why would we?"

He was surprised. "Well, your top investigator, surely he has been given authorization."

They looked at each other, then Brandon. "No, I don't," the investigator confirmed.

"No one in the Public Defender's office has even a classified clearance. I'm not even sure if the U.S. attorneys or Judge Jones have security clearances," Steve said.

Brandon looked at them and marveled at the irony of the situation. "Isn't that something? Here I am, probably the only guy on this floor granted a top secret clearance,[1] and they can't tell me what they know or if it's even classified. Maybe they need to provide the information to me so I can designate the appropriate classification, debrief them, and determine who has a need to know." Having made the remark, they grinned at one another, recognizing the rare levity and ridiculousness of the unusual circumstances.

As they were all standing there, the judge's clerk knocked on the door and said the judge requested their presence back in the courtroom. They were hoping something positive might come out of the surprise revelation by the U.S. attorneys, but the judge said, to their chagrin, "Thank you for your patience. In respect to this, the presently classified information, or at least potentially classified information, is not of such a caliber that would justify immediate release of the material witness. So instead of having a deadline of five tonight, we will call in the grand jury, have them available Friday afternoon, and schedule the material witness's appearance before the grand jury." And like that, it was over.

After the Public Defenders met briefly with the U.S. attorneys, they said Brandon would need to make a final decision: either he would agree to a deposition by the government with limited immunity or he would invoke his Fifth Amendment right at the grand jury hearing scheduled for Friday and face possible contempt or indictment. Brandon answered that it was a very weighty decision and he wanted to discuss it with Mona, if possible, before giving them an answer. They told him they would try and make arrangements to have her available the next morning if the judge allowed it, but with or without her he needed to make a decision.

Brandon was escorted back to the jail cell in the customary fashion, with chains, and doors, and holding cells, and frisks, and searches, and strange and scary voices, and screams and groans and echoes of slamming doors. He ruminated on the day's emotional roller coaster and collapsed onto his plastic pad as soon as he entered his cell. Lying in bed, though, he hesitated to fall asleep. Usually, he would have no reservation, but he had one prayer left for the day and he felt guilty not doing it. He pulled himself up and prayed the night prayer. It was the first day he had prayed a full five times in a single day. He was spent and had no energy left. He could not fight anymore. All he could do was pray for a miracle—or at least strength to endure.

§ § §

[1] Brandon received the clearance while in the military.

Chapter 19
Silent Light

"Light Light The visible reminder of Invisible Light." T.S. Eliot.

Early the next morning the guards woke Brandon, telling him he needed to go to the federal courthouse. The transfer was earlier than the previous court appearances which made him nervous. He was placed in the holding cell at the courthouse, then about half an hour later he was placed in the visiting room where arrangements had been made for him to meet with Mona to discuss his options. A long time passed, and Mona did not show up. He wondered if the judge had denied him the visit and if he would be forced to make the decision himself. What a cruel false sense of hope they gave him. As he was agonizing over how he would take his certain poison, Steve and Chris entered the other side of the visiting room. He was not expecting them.

They both looked at him as if something big had just happened, almost uncontained. Brandon asked them in anguish, "Guys, where's Mona? I thought I was going to get to talk to her."

"Don't worry. She is in the courtroom upstairs right now as we speak. We're headed up there in just a minute, but there is something we need to tell you." Brandon wanted to tell them he needed more time, that he had not made his decision yet. He worried they were there to tell him he could not meet with Mona.

That's when they said it—the most pleasant sentence ever spoken to Brandon. The answer to his prayers. The vindication he thought he would never get. The ticket to his freedom.

"We just got through talking to the U.S. attorney's office, and they told us of their intention to file a motion for your release." The words escaped Steve's lips like honey through a sieve—slow, sweet, and heavy. Brandon let it sink in, as if undeserving of such good news. The mere thought of freedom at that point was incomprehensible. He had just the day before resigned to a long imprisonment.

He could feel a lump forming in his throat. "What do you mean release?" he asked incredulously. Was it a mistake? Another cruel joke? What could have possibly changed since the previous day?

"The government was recently informed, we can't say exactly when, by the Spanish Police that they have positively identified the print that the FBI believed was yours in fact belongs to a Spanish Algerian named Daoud Ounani. The news first hit the papers in Spain and is, even now as we speak, just starting to spread to every major media outlet in the U.S. and throughout the world."

"But what about the FBI's so called 100% identification?" Brandon asked.

Steve shook his head in disbelief. "Brandon, we don't know at this point. We're as surprised as you are. We just know that the government currently is moving for your release and that's been our primary goal from day one."

Brandon looked at them through welling eyes, and with an unmistakable, slack-jaw "see, I told you it wasn't me" expression, cracked a smile. It was an ethereal moment. As quick as hell had fallen on his shoulders it was lifted off, and he could feel the choking of injustice loosening its grip.

"So that's it. They knew all along that the Spanish police were having doubts that the fingerprint belonged to me but decided to detain me." Brandon said absently, talking to himself loudly enough for the others to hear. "They continued their investigation and searches of me and my papers and belonging when I had absolutely nothing to do with what happened over there. Only now that the Spanish Police announce to the whole world that they have identified the individual with the real fingerprint matching the one on the bag...only now does the government decide to release me." He felt both insulted and redeemed.

As Brandon was taken up to the courtroom in shackles and chains by the U.S. marshals for the last time, one of the older marshals, who he recognized had been present for most of the proceedings, looked at Brandon in bewilderment and remarked, "You know, based on what went on here these last couple of weeks, somebody ought to write a book about it." Brandon wanted to reach out and hug the man, the first to see him on his way to freedom. People were coming to their senses. They knew he was not a terrorist. Brandon nodded, barely there. "Yeah, I think you're right, somebody should. Maybe I will, but I'm not sure if anyone would believe it."

Soon the whole world would know of his innocence.

§ § §

The U.S. attorneys addressed the court. "Your Honor. Basically, the Spanish government has informed us they have identified latent print number 17, which the FBI lab and the Court expert had matched to Mr. Mayfield's prints, as belonging to another individual in Spain. At this point the FBI lab is awaiting the information from Spain so they can make a thorough examination of the second person's fingerprints and tell us what the situation is—it is still our opinion that it is Mr. Mayfield's print on that blue bag." The FBI would not admit its blunder. "But in light of this information, it is our request that Mr. Mayfield be released pending further action in this material witness proceeding, but that he be subject to electronic monitoring, home detention, and posting of bond of the money that was found in the safety deposit box."

Chris, in response, said that the money the government confiscated in the safety deposit box was from Mona's inheritance from her father and was the only money they had to survive on because it was their only source of income and any pending clientele had been forced to go to other lawyers.

The judge granted the government's motions, except the electronic monitoring request, and ordered Brandon's release. He then addressed Brandon directly. "Mr. Mayfield, as an officer of the court and as a person who has defended people, you should not be making any comments concerning the merits of this case—this is an ongoing process. If you are right, eventually you will be completely exonerated. At that time you can tell the world anything you want." Brandon wanted to shout at the whole world that his fingerprint was not on the blue bag, but he pursed his lips tautly and listened on. "But until that time you are still a material witness. You are still under a gag order with the exception of what I have approved. We don't know if you will be completely released as a material witness, or whether eventually you might be indicted on the basis of validating fingerprints and other matters that you are engaged in. So, do you follow what I'm saying?"

Brandon answered gratefully, "Yes, your Honor."

Then he asked Brandon, "How do you feel about that?"

The free but shackled man answered diplomatically "I am following you, your Honor. I respect the dignity you have afforded me under these unusual circumstances here, the detention facility here in Multnomah County, and you facilitating my ability to communicate with my clients on a limited basis. I want to thank you for that." He paused before his request. "I understand what you are saying. The only thing I might ask on the condition of my release is that I have children that go to school. I would like to continue taking them to school." The judge approved.

"You can take him to the back room, or you can get him changed in there and then go straight out—Steve, he can go straight out here," Judge Jones said as he pointed to the staff entrance and not the inmate's entrance. The Judge then instructed the marshals to bring Brandon his things and had him give basic information to the parole officer from pre-trial services. As Brandon was signing papers for pre-trial services and waiting for his clothes to arrive, he could hardly contain himself knowing that he was just moments away from walking out of the courtroom and into the light.

The same marshal who removed his chains for the last time handed Brandon the clothes that he had on the day he was arrested. It was as though he had been in a suspended animation for two weeks and was resuming where he left off, with the same clothes and on the same day of the week. Brandon asked where his ring and wallet were, but the marshal wasn't sure and said he would try to track them down. He also handed Brandon his belongings that were gathered from back in his cell, including the Koran and prayer rug. Brandon clutched the Koran and rug firmly in one hand, a symbol of hope and light for a man who was emerging from an indescribable darkness. He went to hug Mona who was waiting for him smiling in the back of the courtroom. He changed his clothes and took the judge's elevator for the first time, along with Judge Jones, Mona, several federal marshals, and the Public Defenders to the lobby of the federal courthouse on the ground floor below.

When the elevator doors opened onto the lobby, he could see bright beautiful beams of natural light cascading in from the glass menagerie in the foyer, radiating crisp, clean, and silently, in stark contrast to the artificial glow and hum of the fluorescent lights he had become accustomed to. Outside of the glass he could clearly see a small army of reporter's amassed on the steps leading up to the courthouse. Steve led Brandon to the glass doors exiting the courthouse and let him go out first.

Brandon squinted and blinked from the bright warm light of the sun and the popping and whirring of camera flashes as the crews and reporters moved in closer. They put their foam covered microphones right up to his face, some kneeling and others standing, jockeying for the best position and anxiously waiting for Brandon to make a comment. He took a deep breath and said. "I want to thank my friends and family for their support in what I'll call a harrowing ordeal." As he was about to continue, unexpectedly Kent, Tonya, and Brandon's three children came up right behind him, made a hole through the wall of reporters and stared in disbelief. Brandon gave Kent a warm brotherly embrace and felt overjoyed at the sight of his kids. He could not have been happier.

Brandon hugged his children and then held up the Koran that he had been tightly clutching ever since he left the courtroom and gave it a kiss. "I want to thank the Multnomah County Detention Center for this lovely Holy Koran."

Finally, standing there on the steps of the courthouse without shackles on his feet, the beautiful broad daylight shining all around him, having miraculously emerged from the clutches of darkness, as a living witness to God's infinite power and mercy, the only other thing he had to add, was first in Arabic with emphasis, "Allahoo Ahkbar, Lay Ilaha Ilahla," then slowly and deliberately in English, "God is great. There is no god but God."

§ § §

On May 20, after Spain had identified latent print #17 as belonging to an Algerian named Daoud Ounani, the U.S. government moved for Brandon's release.[1] The next day the FBI dispatched two fingerprint examiners to Madrid to look at the original and examine the prints of the Algerian, but apparently they only looked at another photograph of the fingerprint when they were there because the original had mysteriously been destroyed.[2] Initially the government explained the mistake based on a poor quality copy of latent print #17.[3] If the original was destroyed during the lifting of the print, then Spain's copy, which was presumably better, could have been accessed from as early as March 13, 2004 when a copy was forwarded to Virginia. Also, the suggestion by the government that it was working on an inferior copy of the print is inconsistent with its 15-point plus 100% positive identification.

In a congressional briefing regarding the mishap, the FBI told members of Congress that it came up with a match after working off a second generation digital copy (a copy of a copy).[4] Later, it gave conflicting responses in interviews to the New York Times saying they were uncertain what generation the digital prints represented.[5]

To further muddy the water, Attorney General John Ashcroft testified before the Senate Judiciary Committee on June 8 and said, "The fingerprint had been a photograph from a partial print. And obviously when the real print became available and additional analysis was engaged in, it was determined [that it was a match]." [6]

This begs the question how the FBI could have taken a photograph of only part of the print and been able to find 15 points of similarity to Brandon's print while the Spanish Police were able to find only 7 points.

The assertion that the FBI was working from a substandard print was contradicted by Allan Bayle, a fingerprint examiner who had worked for Scotland Yard for 25 years. The Federal Public Defender, immediately following Brandon's release, enlisted the advice of Mr. Bayle, who is regarded by many as one of the best fingerprint examiners in the world. With respect to the misidentifications made by the FBI fingerprint and court-appointed examiners, Bayle noted, "There were many discrepancies. A competent expert should have seen all the discrepancies." [7] Bayle also derided the examiners, saying, "The clarity of a photo of the Madrid print, lifted from a plastic bag of detonators found in a stolen van near a train station after the bombings, is good, and no competent examiner should have called it a match." [8]

The Attorney General's office and the LPU initially refused to exclude Mayfield even though they were aware that latent print #17 as well as two other prints on the blue bag were positively identified as belonging to the right hand of Daoud.[9]

A January 7, 2006, review by the Office of the Inspector General—the Justice Department's internal watchdog—found that FBI fingerprint experts had made numerous mistakes in identifying the print as belonging to Mayfield during the investigation of the 2004 Madrid train bombings. Among other things, the Inspector General found the FBI experts overlooked "important differences" between the prints and "the FBI Laboratory's overconfidence in the skill and superiority of its examiners prevented it from taking the [Spanish report] as seriously as it should have." [10]

The report revealed that the examiners engaged in circular reasoning. After finding 10 points of similarity between Mayfield's fingerprint and the fingerprint found on the bag of detonators, "the FBI examiners began to 'find' additional features in [the fingerprint on the bag] that were not really there, but rather were suggested to the examiners by features in the Mayfield prints." [11] Sloppy execution in the ACE-V procedure is common. According to the procedure, analysis and comparison steps are to be done separately with a detailed description of the mark being made before an examiner ever sees the comparison print. This is done to prevent the discovery of previously unnoticed features in the suspect's prints. To save time, many examiners do the two steps together, contributing to the circular reasoning identified in the Mayfield case. [12]

A revealing experiment was done by cognitive neuroscientist Itiel Dror and fingerprint examiner Dave Charlton, in which five international fingerprint analysts were given the same fingerprint twice but received different information about the case each time. The experts were told they were seeing the erroneously matched fingerprints of Brandon Mayfield. This was done to influence what the expert determinations would be since most experts were aware it was a misidentification. What they were actually provided were fingerprints from other cases where they had made determinations years before. Nearly all of the test subjects changed their minds. [13]

Despite denying that the examiners "were improperly influenced by knowledge of Mayfield's religion when they made the identification," [14] the Inspector General's Report makes it clear that Mayfield's unique identity as a Muslim and his experience defending an alleged terrorist in a child custody case were damning considerations. "One of the examiners candidly admitted that if the person identified had been someone without these characteristics, like the 'Maytag repairman,' the laboratory might have revisited the identification with more skepticism and caught the error." [15] The report also conceded that "…the increased information sharing allowed by the Patriot Act amplified the consequences of the FBI's fingerprint misidentification."[16]

In response to the Inspector General's report and recommendations, the Latent Print Unit (LPU) conducted its own investigation. To date the LPU does not use standard blind testing in all of its examinations, leaving the errors that happened in the Mayfield case to occur again and again. Also, the FBI announced in a 2006 Justice Department report that, as result of the errors in the Mayfield case, it began to review the cases of all state and federal prisoners scheduled for execution to determine whether bureau fingerprint examiners made errors that led to death sentences, apparently finding no mistakes.

Very few other scientific fields would ever consider non-blind testing procedures, yet it remains routine for fingerprint identification. The examination of Mayfield's prints was made on the unregulated interpretations of the examiners, not on set standards and protocols. John Massey, an agent with over 30 years' experience, said in an interview with the Chicago Tribune that he and his fellow examiners had done their job and nothing more.[17] He admitted that he knew in examining Mayfield prints that the other examiner had already identified the print as a match. In spite of this and the mistake, he insisted, "I'll preach fingerprints till I die. They're infallible."[18]

Something more than standardization and blind review, however, needs to be adopted and implemented. Instead of a set number of points (which is better than no agreed upon number for identification as it currently stands), identifications should be made on the basis of probabilities. The analysis stage needs to be full analysis where you stop, describe, and then annotate with no changing afterwards. Then you do the same thing with the latent print before you do your comparison. Then if there are differences you cannot go back and tweak the data to say this is what I saw. There should be blind comparison as well as blind verification. The examiner should not have any background information on the suspect whose print they are examining or crime that is being investigated (for example, in Manchester as in many British police forces the forensic division is separate, whereas in the U.S. most of the work is done in the same police department).

There has to be more data admitting error rates or limits of actual identical matches. For example, there can be small minute changes in one's own prints for various reasons over time. Children do not exert the oil that we do, so their prints are generally not as reliable or as easy to capture.[19] Identifications should be postulated in terms of percentages rather than as identification, exclusion, or inconclusive.[20] Additionally there need to be rules regarding usefulness of partial prints or simultaneous prints. Until this happens, more innocent people will be exposed to possible wrongful conviction based on evidence that has historically been viewed as infallible when in fact it is very useful, but still very subjective. Although the Mayfield case highlights the problems and limits of current fingerprint forensics, it's important to note that the bias made in the fingerprint examination was symptomatic of a larger institutionalized effort to target and profile ethnic and religious minorities without probable cause.

The Spanish Police's independent analysis of Mayfield's print, and its refusal to cave into the FBI's intense pressure to wrongly identify him, helped save him from prosecution and the possible capital punishment conviction he was facing. As Steve Wax put it, "But for the unusual circumstance of another national police agency conducting its own independent investigation, Mr. Mayfield would still be incarcerated." And as Chris Schatz wondered, "Who knows how many people are sitting in state and federal prisons that have just never come to light because there is no independent agency like the Spanish National Police."[21]

§ § §

[1] Kershaw, Sarah. "Spain and U.S. at Odds on Mistaken Terror Arrest." *The New York Times*. The New York Times, 5 June 2004. Web. 29 Aug. 2014. <http://www.nytimes.com/2004/06/05/us/spain-and-us-at-odds-on-mistaken-terror-arrest.html?module=Search&mabReward=relbias%3Ar>

[2-5] *Id.*

[6] *See* "Text: Ashcroft Comments on Anti-Terror Policy." Washington Post. The Washington Post. Web. 25 Sept. 2014. <http://www.washingtonpost.com/wp-dyn/articles/A25211-2004Jun8.html>.

[7] Wax, Steven T., and Christopher J. Schatz. "A Multitude of Errors: The Brandon Mayfield Case." Champion Magazine. 1 Oct. 2004. Web. 25

Sept. 2014. <http://www.nlada.org/Defender/forensics/for_lib/ Documents/1107541411.93/>

[8] Heath, David. "FBI's handling of fingerprint case criticized." The Seattle Times. 4 June 2004. Web. 25 Sept. 2014. <http://seattletimes.com/ html/localnews/2001944007_fingerprint01m.html>

[9] "A Review of the FBI's Handling of the Brandon Mayfield Case." U.S. Department of Justice. Office of the Inspector General, March 2006. Web. 29 Aug. 2014. 90-92. <http://www.justice.gov/oig/special/s0601/ final.pdf>

[10] *Id.*

[11] *Id.* at 7.

[12] Spinney, Laura. "Science in Court: The Fine Print." Nature.com. Nature Publishing Group, 17 Mar. 2010. Web. 6 Nov. 2014. <http:// www.nature.com/news/2010/100317/full/464344a.html>

[13] See, e.g., Itiel E. Dror et al., Contextual Information Renders Experts Vulnerable to Making Erroneous Identifications, 156 FORENSIC SCI. INT'L 74 (2006) Itiel E. Dror & David Charlton, Why Experts Make Errors, 56 J. FORENSIC IDENTIFICATION 600 (2006);

[14] Supra note 9 at 11.

[15] *Id.* at 179.

[16] *Id.* at 267.

[17] Tangen, Jason M.. "Identification personified." Australian Journal of Forensic Sciences 45.3 (2013): 1. Taylor and Francis Group. Web. 25 Sept. 2014.

[18] *Id.*

[19] Ashbaugh, David R. "Ridgeology" (PDF). Royal Canadian Mounted Police. Retrieved 2013-10-26. Available at http://onin.com/fp/ridgeology.pdf.

[20] For a good primer regarding the need for and challenges regarding probabilistic matches, see Cole, Simon. "More than Zero: Accounting for Error in Latent Fingerprint Identification." The Journal of Criminal Law & Criminology 95.3 (2005). Print.

[21] Sherrer, Hans. "That's Not My Fingerprint, Your Honor." *Denied* 1 June 2004: 11, *available at* <http://justicedenied.org/issue/issue_25/ jd_issue_25.pdf>

Epilogue

After Brandon was released, he was placed on house arrest for another week before all restrictions were lifted. Based on the government's admitted misidentification and its own motion to dismiss, the judge dismissed the material witness proceedings against Brandon and ordered the government to return all property and papers it seized. The judge also lifted the gag order he had placed on Brandon and allowed him to talk to the public for the first time. Brandon explained briefly his ordeal, the humiliation and embarrassment he had to endure, the damage it had done to his practice and reputation, and of course that he was profiled for being a Muslim. "I believe I was singled out and discriminated against. I feel, as a Muslim, people should wake up. We need to start protecting our civil liberties," he said. "The material witness statute obviously gives the government too much power and must be amended, if not repealed...This shouldn't happen to anybody. If it's not the Muslims today it could easily be you tomorrow if we do not stand up and object to what's going on right now."

The same day he first spoke publicly, the FBI did something it rarely ever does. It apologized. It was a public statement, not to Brandon or his family personally, but an apology nonetheless: "The FBI apologizes to Mr. Mayfield and his family for the hardships that this matter has caused."[1] Sorry was good and a commendable first step, but sorry would not undo the extensive damage that the government had caused to him and his family, nor would it resolve the untold devastation it was causing and would continue to cause countless others. Sorry was not good enough. Sorry did not explain what had gone wrong.

The U.S. Attorney's Office offered to make a personal apology to Brandon, but only on the condition that he admitted he was not targeted as a Muslim—an offer which Brandon naturally refused. Initially, he and Tom Nelson made an informal offer to settle the damages for $50,000.00 dollars, for which the government refused.

In the weeks and months that followed, the Mayfields' conversations were guarded. Any intimate moments were avoided, with the prospect of cameras watching or monitoring devices listening. The family could no longer be certain that Big Brother was not still watching them. The kids' grades suffered, as did their sense of safety and wellbeing. Brandon and Mona became depressed and despondent. The work at the office dropped off. Some clients would not meet with him in his office, believing it to be bugged by the federal government. Some immigration clients actually met with him only in nearby coffee shops for this reason. One prospective family law client would not meet with him because she thought he, as a Muslim, beat and oppressed women. Still others went to him, or other local attorneys made referrals and gave words of support out of both pity and kindness.

People throughout the country sent letters of encouragement or just said they were sorry that the government did what it did. But some letters and calls were disturbing, discriminatory, hateful, and even threatening. One caller from Florida suggested Brandon go back to Iraq with his wife for representing those terrorists who murdered so many innocent Americans on September 11. Another caller left several messages that could not be traced, repeatedly calling Mr. Mayfield "a piece of shit." Others just sent e-mails calling him, his family, and all Muslims every derogatory explicative profanity imaginable. These calls, letters, and messages, caused the family an added sense of fear, insult, and apprehension in addition to that which the government had already inflicted.

Brandon was becoming increasingly critical of the administration and was beginning to piece together a picture of a government within a government, a secret agenda operating under the guise of a public policy. For a variety of reasons he was beginning to understand he was the perfect patsy. Knowing the media was not interested in finding the truth and the government not in a hurry to correct itself, he also knew the government had misused the material witness statute and that key provisions of the Patriot Act and FISA were unconstitutional. Out of frustration, he tried to reach out to someone who might help, upon the advice of a friend he had worked with in Newport.

Brandon flew to Salt Lake City and from there took a small twin engine charter plane to Jackson Hole. Turbulent clouds persisted all the way from

Utah to Wyoming. Just as he started to make the bumpy descent for the final approach to Jackson Hole the clouds parted with a stunning view of the jagged peaks of the grand Tetons and its ancient glacier valleys dotted with countless moraine and alpine lakes sparkling like diamonds whenever the sun reflected off their surface. There he met the attorney who would eventually admit he wanted to tear off the government's head and shove it down their throat—Gerry Spence, perhaps the most reputable American trial attorney since Clarence Darrow.

At the small airport Brandon was greeted by Gerry's personal assistant who drove him to his motel room to check in, then on to Gerry's cabin over the Snake River and through the pine and birch covered woods. Gerry greeted Brandon at the front door of his cabin and waved him in as he fended off the dogs. He was quite tall, taller than Brandon imagined. Not a towering figure, just tall, with long gray hair, rough angular features, and a penetrating look. He asked if Brandon wanted something to drink, then Brandon proceeded to follow him to his office upstairs. It was more of a quiet den, probably for writing or reflecting. The walls were covered with a few furs and a sparse collection of various art work, mostly in a Native American early pioneer motif.

"I know you're a successful trial lawyer, but do you know anything about the Patriot Act, the Material Witness Statute, and the Foreign Intelligence Surveillance Act? Are you up to speed on these areas?" Brandon asked.

Gerry looked at Brandon, tilted his head, and answered in a soft deep voice, the way parents talk to their children who don't know better. "Brandon, if you're bankrupt who do you go to? You go to a bankruptcy attorney. If you have a tax problem who do you go to?"

"I suppose a tax attorney" he reflected.

"That's right, you go to an accountant or a tax attorney. But what if you're bringing a complaint against the federal government and its agents in a case that will be brought before a jury? Who do you want to represent you?" He did not answer so Gerry answered for him. "A bankruptcy attorney in the courtroom couldn't find his ass with his hands. I can find somebody who knows something about FISA and the Patriot Act and civil rights, and I can find my way around in a courtroom. You get my point?" Brandon nodded.

Brandon was never provided a copy of the secret search and seizure warrants used to monitor him. Later, however, the government confirmed that in his home and office, it had secretly inspected and photographed over 200 items and documents, made mirror images of hard drives, rummaged through the trash, bugged and monitored their home including private conversations between husband and wife and parents and children, took DNA swabs, hair samples, nail clippings, and even cigarette butts.

But with all their snooping, break-ins and spying, they still could not find any evidence of wrongdoing aside from the alleged fingerprint match.

Gerry, with the help of someone who did know something about FISA and the Patriot Act, Elden Rosenthal, and an old friend from Newport, Michele Longer Eder, agreed to represent the Mayfield family.

In October of 2004, Mr. Mayfield and his family, with his attorneys' assistance, filed a complaint against the U.S. government for wrongful arrest and unauthorized search and surveillance of their home and his law office in Portland, Oregon. In November of 2006 they settled the financial damages portion of the complaint, including charges of wrongful arrest and imprisonment for a respectable two million dollars. The settlement agreement required that the family would be able to continue to challenge the constitutionality of the key provisions of the Patriot Act.

On September 26, 2007, Judge Aiken of the Federal District Court ruled that the two key FISA provisions they challenged, as amended by the Patriot Act, permitted the government to conduct surveillance and searches targeting Americans without satisfying the required probable cause standard in the Fourth Amendment.

"Prior to the amendments [to FISA], the three branches of government operated with thoughtful and deliberate checks and balances—a principle upon which our nation was founded," Aiken wrote.

But the Patriot Act, she said, eliminated "the constitutionally required interplay between executive action, judicial decision, and Congressional enactment."

"For over 200 years, this nation has adhered to the rule of law—with unparalleled success. A shift to a nation based on extra-constitutional authority is prohibited, as well as ill-advised," she wrote.

The government appealed the decision, which was overturned by a three judge panel sitting for the ninth circuit, finding Brandon Mayfield did not have standing because, even if they ruled in his favor, the courts could not redress the harm (i.e. get back or have destroyed all derivative material because the government might choose not to obey the order). Their petition to the U.S. Supreme Court was denied, leaving the determination for another day.

§ § §

Brandon and Mona found it too unbearable to stay in the same home (and law office). They moved to a different home in 2006 and to a different office in 2008. They continue to live and work in Oregon. The kids are now all grown up and on their own. Shane is married with children and in the Army National Guard, Sharia currently attends Georgetown Law and works part-time in the Senate as an Intelligence Advisor, and Samir is working and going to school part time while managing to make music in his free time. Mona and Brandon still work together and run the law office.

Over the last 10 years, with few exceptions, the majority of decisions by the Supreme Court, acts of Congress, and executive authority have upheld those policies adopted to implement the government's new war on terror, even when those policies seem to clearly contravene time honored constitutional rights and protections.

The previous administration and Congress, by adopting rules and policies to implement the war on terror, operated on the premise that it is better to be secure than free. The current administration and Congress, by continuing to implement and support those policies, has *de facto* also agreed that it is indeed better to be secure than free.

The President, although understanding that our values are our greatest security asset and that recent policies have undermined both our security and liberty, has been, with the exception of his order to end torture and his push to get out of Iraq, mostly ineffective in altering the trend of diminishing civil rights and the rise of executive police powers globally, nationally, and locally. He has yet to close Guantanamo Bay, and his administration has failed to investigate specific instances of torture, continued warrantless surveillance and military tribunals, killed U.S. citizens deemed to be terrorist, retained the authority to carry out extraordinary renditions, and has blocked dozens of public interest lawsuits challenging privacy violations and Presidential abuses.

§ § §

[1] "Statement on Brandon Mayfield Case." FBI. 24 May 2004. Web. 25 Sept. 2014. <http://www.fbi.gov/news/pressrel/press-releases/statement-on-brandon-mayfield-case>.

Words from Brandon Mayfield

My brother Kent, an art teacher from the Midwest, on Sunday May 9, 2004, three days after I was arrested, while I was sitting in jail with no communication between myself and my family, summed up the then current state of affairs best in the following journal entry:

"This is the ugly face of deceit, the manipulation of victim's emotions, lies, fabrication and distortions used for political agendas. Find the truth behind the lies, then realize, they're not so wise. Our enemies are real, and in fact they're everywhere. Ingrained into our great society, corrupt organizations bloom violently, feeding on fear, fasting on morality. But the disease on the congressional spine can be cured."

That was over 10 years ago. Where are we now? Today, in 2015, we are living in 1984. I don't mean 1984, the year I graduated high school and decided to join the army to support and defend our constitution. I am talking about George Orwell's frightening brave new world order in which Big Brother is constantly watching you, complete with 24 hour surveillance, thought control, and "newspeak" or double speak. Where war means peace, freedom is slavery, ignorance is strength. Where torture is morality and an act that strips you of your civil rights is called a Patriot Act. Where a war of aggression and occupation could be called "Operation Infinite Freedom." Like the men and women of Oceana, we the people, living under the government's lies and propaganda for so long, have forgotten how to enjoy the simple pleasure of life.

I sometimes think back to those high school days of my 1984 with fond memories, and of how fortunate I was to live in a country that valued freedom, individuality, and creativity. A world in which every rural high school had a well-funded art and music department as well as a track and football field, and the only thing you had to pay for to participate was the price of your own shoes or paint brushes. A day when voicing your displeasure to the government's excesses was the American Way, not a label of suspicion and subversion.

But I have other more recent not so pleasant memories, such as my anger and frustration with the systematic and incremental erosion of our civil liberties with the passing of the Material Witness Statute in 1984, the Omnibus Counter Terrorism Act of 1995, the Patriot Act of 2001, and the Military Commission Act of 2006. All this whittling away at our civil liberties with a conversely increasing growth of our secret government, secret services, CIA, FBI, NSA, and now Homeland Security. And by the way—secret government, and secret agencies, means no accountability.

I remember my dismay and shame when our administration declared a pre-emptive war on the pretext of a lie, that Iraq had weapons of mass destruction, and invaded and bombed, with "Shock and Awe," an innocent civilian population that killed hundreds of thousands, fomented a bitter civil war, and will continue to disrupt the lives of millions more for decades to come.

All for foreign oil, growth of the Military Industrial Complex, and justification of the Capitalist Corporate War Machine. Those who would stand in the way of the machine risk getting thrown under its wheels—people such as Captain James Yee, the military chaplain at Guantanamo Bay, accused of spying, his name and reputation smeared, only to have the charges dropped. Lieutenant Ehrin Watada, an exemplary soldier who refused to serve in Iraq on moral grounds that it was an unjust war, but who would have served anywhere else. Lynne Stewart, the civil rights attorney, who defended her Muslim client too zealously. Edward Snowden for exposing the infrastructure of our massive surveillance state. Finally, those wrongfully accused of terror, such as Kareem Koubriti, Abdel El-Mardoudi, Sami Al Husseyn, and Osama Awadallah—and the list goes on and on.

I have dark memories of my own stifling paranoia of being monitored, watched, tracked, bugged, surveilled, followed, and targeted, primarily for my religious affiliation as a practicing Muslim, and for simply doing my job, which is to help defend others who cannot defend themselves—to give them a right to be heard and have their day in court.

To a man with a hammer everything and everyone appears to be a nail. So too with the NSA, FBI, and CIA. If we wanted to be 100 percent safe and if we completely trusted the government, we would check in and share with law investigation officials on a daily basis, informing them of our whereabouts, activities, comings and goings, and who we associated with and what we saw. In turn they would screen this information and follow up on any potentially imminent threats to us or others and would share with other law enforcement officials details of any potential criminal activity.

Today, with the advent of the internet and wireless communications, we do not have to report daily to law investigation officials; they secretly come to us and pour over our data, communications, conversations, pictures, videos, purchases, correspondences, inquiries, interests, and associations on a daily basis. The NSA does it primarily with electronic intercept and bulk metadata collection, the FBI and CIA with a combination of undercover agents and informants (often paid criminals, local or international), physical searches and surveillance, as well as electronic intercept.

Edward Snowden, a thoughtful, soft spoken young NSA analyst, with little to gain and much to lose, said something very important that we should pay close attention to if we value our autonomy, privacy, and freedom:[1]

"Even if you are not doing anything wrong you are being watched and recorded...You don't have to have done anything wrong, you simply have to eventually fall under suspicion from somebody—even by a wrong call, and then they can use this system to go back in time and scrutinize every decision you have ever made, every friend you have ever discussed something with, and attack you on that basis..."

Guilt by association and circumstances is an ugly but currently fashionable thing in certain intelligence circles. In the case of myself and family, the government revealed that they had evidence of Spanish travel documents which turned out to be my middle-school daughter Sharia's Spanish homework assignment. They had evidence of target practice: my 15 year-old son Shane had browsed online for an Airsoft pistol. The affidavit in support of my arrest cited that I had advertised in a Middle East yellow pages (a directory that G.E. and major car rental agencies also advertise in) and that I had called or been called by a number listed for a Southern Oregon mosque and director of an Islamic charity that was under federal investigation (later the charity was taken off OFAC's naughty list and local director, Pete Seda, was cleared of any terrorist activities).

These innocent activities were characterized as ominous circumstantial evidence of involvement in a major terrorist bomb plot. If not for the Spanish Police's insistence that the fingerprint found at the site of the Madrid bombing was not mine, I cannot say with confidence I would be alive to share with you my experiences today.

Former administrations and congressmen argued that there was a wall between intelligence gathering and law enforcement that required special measurers and tools to bring down that wall. The tools that they crafted to bring down that enormously exaggerated wall include legislation such as the Patriot Act. But the real wall, the strong wall set in bedrock for centuries, was the wall protecting us from tyranny and unchecked governmental power.

That wall was the Fourth Amendment. That clause, since this country's inception, has been interpreted to mean that probable cause that a crime has been committed must exist before conducting any searches or seizures. Any warrantless wiretaps, or warranted wiretaps, or orders without probable cause and specificity, are forms of search of us and our papers and effects and in violation of the Fourth Amendment.

Yet on May 6, 2004, I was arrested without probable cause that I had committed a crime, under the material witness statute, and was told by the U.S. Attorney's Office, after several days of pouring through my client files and personal papers, they had enough to charge me, just not enough to convict me yet, for a crime punishable by death. They used my detention and search of my home and office as a means to gather mass amounts of information that they otherwise would not have had access to, information to build a case even where none existed.

There is a reason why we have the Fourth Amendment—to codify the difference between suspicion and probable cause. Suspicion is when you have a hunch. Under the Fourth Amendment that is not enough to invade our privacy. The Fourth Amendment should not be negotiable unless Congress wants to propose a constitutional amendment to rescind it. If such an amendment were suggested, however, I suspect the American people would run our Senators and Representatives out of office upon the hint of such a scurrilous proposal. The problem is that Congress and the Executive branch, without such an amendment, are passing laws in violation of the Fourth Amendment repeatedly and infringing on our rights so frequently that the warrant and probable cause requirements are becoming virtually meaningless. That bastion of protection against overreaching government intrusion is being dismantled piece by piece to its very foundation.

Fortunately, we have some Senators and Representatives that still look out for the rights of the American people. Take Senator Ron Wyden, for example, who had been warning for years that if we only knew what he was not authorized to divulge we would be shocked. He appears to have been alluding to the monstrous data collection and phone monitoring program that Edward Snowden leaked information about to the Guardian. When Senator Wyden questioned James Clapper, director of the NSA, in March of 2013 as to whether the NSA collects any type of data on millions of Americans, Clapper responded point blank, "No."

That is a bold faced lie to a long term U.S. Senator by the head of a secret agency. And that is a lesson in allowing growth of secret sectors of government. By the nature of their secrecy there is little oversight whereby they become emboldened and accountable to virtually no one. This is a classic illustration of the term "democracies die behind closed doors."

Many of the most dangerous policies that right-minded and justice-seeking American citizens warned us about 8, 9, and 10 years ago are still in place. It has recently come to our attention that drones are being used to kill and assassinate foreign nationals and citizens alike for what may be nothing more than violent speech. (By all accounts, Mr. Al-Awlaki, the first U.S. citizen to die in a "secret" drone assassination, was killed primarily for allegations that the messages he was posting were inciting violence such that they posed an imminent threat to the nation's security—but of course he will never have an opportunity to personally answer or respond to such allegations or to present evidence and testimony in his defense).

Just try and fathom, if you will, where we are and where we are heading. Gathering mass amount of data and conversations on virtually every American citizen (soon every individual globally) who uses electronic devices (without warrants or probable cause) and unilateral executive authorization for the execution and death of individuals without due process of law, without charges or judge and jury.

This is the America we live in today, and it has now surpassed even the fantastical oppressive dystopias of Kafka and Orwell. Big Brother is not only watching you and imprisoning you but is starting to assassinate you on secret evidence as well.

I pray that we, unlike Winston of Oceana, do not sell ourselves too cheaply at the interrogation of our tormentors to leave behind our memories, no matter how unpleasant, or our morals.

I implore you collectively to demand our individual rights be respected and to write your congressmen and women and insist they amend or abrogate the Material Witness Statute, FISA, 50 USC 1804 and 1823, sections 207, 213, 215 and 218 of the Patriot Act, the Omnibus Counter Terrorism Act of 1995, NSA warrantless wiretaps, the Military Commissions Act, which strips us of an 800 year old English right to challenge arrests and provides punishment without a judge and jury, executive-ordered assassinations by drone attack, and the continued imprisonment of detainees (most of whom have committed no crimes, and some of whom after 13 years of torture, humiliation, and degradation, are still without an opportunity to challenge release from their cages).

It is time we see past the deceit and lies of those special interests that have led this great society of ours off course, feeding off of our fear, and have asked us to partake in an unconscionable amendment to our social contract: to trade our liberty for security. We must realize that every legislative law, every executive order, every judicial opinion which undermines our guaranteed rights is one more cornerstone in the construction of an enormous prison system and elaborate police state, the likes of which the world has never seen.

We must then take one brick at a time from our private penitentiaries and detention centers and exchange them one brick at a time into our public schools and hospitals. Our criminal justice system should be used to protect society and reform those for whom we as a society have failed. It is a double injustice to punish and imprison our sick, our poor, and our huddled masses whom we have first failed to heal, to shelter, to educate, or to simply care about. Our justice system must have more mercy and compassion than it gives out punishment and retribution.

It seems there is much work to do, but in the words of Eugene Debbs before a crowd of thousands upon his release from jail for questioning the propriety of our involvement in the First World War, "Eternal Vigilance is the Price of Liberty."

It is my fervent hope that the lessons learned from my case will dispel the myth that fingerprint identification is reliable and that religious profiling is acceptable. Our freedom of religion in this country is a sacred right, and the exercise of one's belief in all lawful manners should never be a factor in a government's investigation of its citizens.

The power of the government to secretly search your home or business without probable cause under the guise of an alleged terrorist investigation or to gather foreign intelligence must be stopped. I look forward to the day the Patriot Act is declared unconstitutional and all citizens and individuals are safe from unwarranted arrests, detentions, and searches by the Federal Government.

Sixty five years ago, Americans kept silent in the belief that encroaching on the rights of a minority preserved America's security. The cost of that silence was the humiliation and alienation of a whole generation of Japanese Americans. We cannot afford to remain silent today.

Sincerely, Brandon Mayfield.

§ § §

[1] Video interview with Edward Snowden. "You're Being Watched."
10 June, 2013. Democracy Now! Available at
http://www.democracynow.org/2013/6/10/
youre_being_watched_edward_snowden_emerges

About the Authors

Sharia Mayfield earned her B.A. in Creative Writing from Stanford University and is currently completing her J.D. at Georgetown University Law Center (after having transferred from the University of Oregon Law School). She has been interviewed by Stanford's KZSU Radio, published in Berkeley's Journal of Comparative Literature, and appeared on Fox Business. Her experience, largely detailed in this book, has propelled her passion to end mass surveillance as well as study national security law and the law of war. In addition to her notorious obsession with privacy law, she enjoys fiction writing and running in her spare time.

Brandon Mayfield, a former Patriot Missile Platoon Leader of the US Army, is a graduate of Washburn University School of Law. He is currently a member of the Oregon State Bar, licensed to practice in federal district courts and the 9th Circuit Court of Appeals, with his emphasis in civil litigation, civil rights, appeals, personal injury, and contracts. He has written on a number of subjects, including governmental profiling of Muslims, the implementation of the War on Terror, and fingerprint forensics, as well as lectured at Yale, Berkeley, Northwestern, and the University of Oregon, among other venues. In addition to writing and lecturing, Brandon has appeared on a number of nationally syndicated news organizations including Fox News, MSNBC, Al Jazeera, and the BBC.

155

Also by Divertir Publishing

Right there, on the gray cinderblock wall, was a jet-black piece of graffiti that I couldn't quite understand at first. Miriam must have caught the look on my face because she explained. "It's a map of Haiti," she said. It made sense suddenly. The map of Haiti had an eye placed in it so that it looked like a face. Coming down from the eye was a single giant tear drop. "Haiti is weeping."

On Tuesday, January 12th 2010, a magnitude 7.0 earthquake shook the island nation of Haiti. The United States Agency for International Development estimated the death toll to be somewhere between 46,000 and 85,000 people, with 220,000 injured and over 1.5 million homeless. Many organizations, both from the U.S. and abroad, responded to the appeal for humanitarian aid.

Dr. Stephen Schroering and Chris Rakunas went to Haiti to deliver over 21,000 pounds of medical and surgical supplies to the New Life Children's Home in Port-au-Prince, Haiti, and several other hospitals. In *Tears for the Mountain*, Chris recounts his mission to deliver these supplies to the earthquake-ravaged island nation. Chris discusses both the triumphs and heartbreaks of the trip, the problems with distributing aid in a nation lacking the most basic infrastructure, and his unexpected encounter with a notorious Haitian warlord.

A portion of the proceeds for this book will be donated to the New Life Children's Home in Port-au-Prince, Haiti.

Visit
http://www.divertirpublishing.com/
for information on this and other titles.

Made in the USA
Middletown, DE
02 January 2017